Perched casually on the arm of John's chair, Cathy leaned over him slightly as he read. What did it take to loosen him up, she wondered. She was sure her closeness bothered him, so it didn't surprise her when John suggested a little stiffly, "Shouldn't you find your own chair?"

"Oh, yeah. Sure."

At last, the math homework was finished. While Cathy slipped the papers back in her book, her fingers accidentally touched John's, and he drew back quickly, as if he'd touched fire. She stole a glance at him and saw that he was red to the roots of his brown hair.

"I guess I'll see you tomorrow," John told her, as they walked to the front door . . .

Something had happened. Cathy had planned to be bored, not interested Math still wasn't interesting, but John was. And he sure wasn't like any of the other boys Cathy knew—which left her pleasantly confused.

The Problem With Love

Rosemary Vernon

BANTAM BOOKS
TORONTO • NEW YORK • LONDON • SYDNEY

RL 6, IL age 11 and up

THE PROBLEM WITH LOVE
A Bantam Book / April 1982
Reprinted 1983

Cover photo by Pat Hill

ISBN 0-553-20787-3

Published simultaneously in the United States and Canada

Bantam Books are published by Bantam Books, Inc. Its trademark, consisting of the words "Bantam Books" and the portrayal of a rooster, is registered in U.S. Patent and Trademark Office and in other countries. Marca Registrada. Bantam Books, Inc., 666 Fifth Avenue, New York, New York 10103.

Printed in Great Britain by Hunt Barnard Printing Ltd.

O 0 9 8 7 6 5 4 3 2 1

This one is for you, Eileen

The Problem With Love

Chapter One

"Here we go!"

Needles of icy spray stung Cathy Meyers' face as the rubber raft plummeted down the American River rapids. The boy sitting next to her, Derek Sorenson, instinctively clamped a hand around Cathy's sun-browned arm while she held onto the aluminum frame for dear life.

It was spring, and the first run of the season for the five life-jacketed teenagers. The river was high because of the melted snow runoff from the Sierra Nevadas, and it was full of debris it had gathered along its route.

Cathy ran her fingers through her tangled, shoulder-length brown hair, dark blue eyes wide with anticipation. She loved the exhilarating rough-and-tumble ride down the river, which carved a roaring path past her hometown. It was a ride that made her scream and laugh, a ride that was always full of surprises.

The five always rode together, with Marty Mason as self-appointed leader of the group, which consisted of himself, Cathy, his sister Jan, Tracy Wilder, and Derek Sorenson. Marty and Jan's family owned the raft, and Marty was one of the best "river rats" there was. He always took great precautions, scouting the river before a run, and he knew how to read the language of the water better than he read his homework assignments. He was one of those single-minded boys who could discuss nothing but white-water sports.

Cathy loved rafting, but she wasn't dedicated to it the way Marty was. In fact, she found it hard to be serious about anything for long. If Cathy was dedicated to anything, it was the idea of trying *everything*—and having fun, ambitions her parents did not value very highly.

Her room at home was littered with roller skates, old ballet shoes, half-finished crafts projects, and dusty paperbacks she'd bought and never read. She had also gone through a period when she had developed a great interest in photography, so her walls were covered with nature photographs she had taken. Some of them had even appeared in the school newspaper. But when she had been asked to join the staff, she had refused. Taking pictures as a job would take all the fun out of it, she decided. Besides, the staff met third period every day, and she didn't want to load up her class schedule. Anyway, by the time they got around to asking her, she had lost interest in photography and found another hobby that took up most of her time and attention—boys.

"We wish you'd be more serious, Cathy," her father often complained. "All you think about these days are boys and parties."

Her standard reply had always been: "Well, you can't complain about my grades, can you? I always manage to get by pretty well, even without studying. There are a lot more interesting things to do than study."

Then came algebra. . . .

Cathy was *not* getting by in algebra. In fact, she was in big trouble. So much trouble that she had done something really dumb. She had told her parents that she had left her report card at school and hadn't had a chance to look at it herself. It was a desperate move to postpone the big scene with her parents until Monday because she had a big weekend planned: the raft trip, a party that night, and skating Sunday. She knew her parents wouldn't have let her out of the house if they had seen her algebra grade.

Still, when she hadn't brought home her report card, the "look" had passed between them—the knowing look that Cathy had learned to read as "we don't believe you."

Ever since Cathy's father had started teaching at her high school, Sierra Heights last fall, substituting for Ms. Curtis in English, Cathy had felt smothered. She had always been fairly popular and had many friends, but with her dad teaching at Sierra, some things had changed.

For instance, now she was categorized as "Mr. Meyers' daughter," Herbie Franklin, who had never had two words to say to her before, now wanted her to smuggle him the answers to her father's English exam. Of course, she had told him to get lost. Eric Merritt wanted to take her out—she found out later that he was hoping to insure himself an A on his report card.

One of her friends had even stopped coming around, finding it difficult to maintain a friendship with Cathy when her father was her English teacher. "I don't know how to act now," Katy Willis complained. "It's so weird being at your house, talking about boys or clothes, with your dad teaching English. I feel like I ought to be discussing prepositional phrases or something. Why don't you come to my house instead?"

"Why should it matter? You never even noticed my father before he was your teacher!" protested Cathy. She was hurt.

Tracy and Jan had tried to console her. "Look, Katy's not your only friend. You've got us. We don't care if your father's a teacher at Sierra."

It was okay for them to say, but when Jan and Tracy ate dinner at Cathy's, they discussed English assignments with her father. School seemed to be invading her whole life.

"Why does it bother you?" Mrs. Meyers questioned. "I think it's wonderful the girls are so interested."

"It bothers me because they're my friends and Daddy is monopolizing the conversation!" Cathy exploded. "We hear enough about schoolwork at school."

"But school is important."

"I'm glad you teach elementary, Mom. I couldn't stand having both of you in the same school with me all day long."

Her mother looked hurt, and Cathy wished she could say things in a nicer way. But it seemed that since school had started in September, she hadn't had a nice thing to say to either of her parents. Of course, she loved them, but having parents who were teachers could really be a drag sometimes, especially when you were in high school.

Always outspoken, Cathy now took the defensive position in every argument. It didn't matter what they talked about. If her parents said the sky was blue, Cathy would insist it was gray. She found herself taking a stand against them even when she knew she was wrong.

To Cathy, her parents seemed dull and set in their ways. All their responses were so well worn that Cathy thought they sounded like a couple of tape recorders. All *they* talked about, it seemed, were grades and education and careers. Cathy couldn't believe that they had ever really *lived* at all. She knew they were happy the way they were, but she couldn't understand how they could be....

"Hey, Cath, are you still with us?" Jan asked, startling Cathy and bringing her back to the present. "How 'bout rowing for a while?"

Cathy accepted reluctantly. She didn't like rowing much, though she'd never say so to her friends. Her oar strokes were shallow and noisy, and she hated the burn in her shoulders after a little steady rowing.

"When you splash like that, you're not getting anywhere," criticized Marty. Marty was a thin, red-haired, freckle-faced boy, and his sister resembled him in hair color and pale skin, minus the freckles.

Tracy smiled. "Cathy's got her own crazy way of doing things. You ought to know that by now, Marty."

"Loony, but an individualist," summarized Marty. "Now just row over to that bank, Cathy, and we'll get out."

"Don't trust my driving, huh?" Cathy joked, maneuvering the raft through the slower water to the bank, where everyone climbed out.

Derek offered her his hand. "How are you getting to the party tonight?"

"Any way I can. Bus, skates, train . . ."

"Okay, smarty. Have it your way." He pretended to sock her in the arm. "I thought you might like to ride with Jan and me."

"Sure. That's the best offer I've had yet." Cathy grinned. She and Derek went out occasionally, but just as friends.

The five teenagers hoisted the raft onto the top of Marty's Dodge van and lashed it onto the rack, then climbed inside.

"Turn on the heater, man, I'm freezing," Derek demanded, through chattering teeth.

"I second the motion," said Tracy.

"I can't wait to take a shower," Cathy muttered, shivering in her soaked cutoffs and bikini top. "Hey, Marty, are you coming to the party? Or are you gonna spend tonight patching the raft?"

The others chuckled. Marty shrugged. "Aw, I might come. It depends."

Marty was the only one of the group who was not social. The other four loved parties.

Cathy leaned between the front seats to talk. "Well, if it wasn't for you, Marty, keeping the raft shipshape, the rest of us wouldn't get to float."

"No kidding, Cathy?" he said, obviously amused. "Without my undying dedication, you would all be up the creek, huh?"

Laughter filled the van as it swung into the Meyers' driveway.

"See you tonight." Cathy jumped out of the van, wearing a thick purple velour towel around her slim waist.

"We'll pick you up," yelled Jan, before Derek slammed the sliding door shut between them.

Cathy ran inside and yelled, "I'm home." After stopping in her bedroom to grab jeans and a plaid shirt, she padded down the tiled hallway to the bathroom, where she turned on the shower full blast. She peeled off her clothes, showered, shampooed her hair, and quickly dressed. Her mother knocked at the door.

"When you get out, your father and I want to talk to you."

Cathy held her breath. Uh-oh. "Okay, Mom." By her mother's tone of voice, she knew she was in trouble. Reluctantly she crept down the hall, on the lookout for her parents.

"Boy are you in the doghouse!" Cathy's thirteen-year-old brother Matt said, as he peered out of his bedroom. In the last year, since he'd entered junior high, Matt had grown from a little stick figure into a broad-shouldered, wisecracking creature one inch taller than Cathy. Cathy teased him about being like their puppy Horace, who had changed from a ball of fur with big feet to a huge red setter with all the right proportions.

"What's up, Matt?" Cathy whispered conspiratorially. The two weren't really close, except when joining forces against their parents.

"Your report card!" he said, rolling his eyes.

"They know?"

"Only about your algebra grade. Marcus spilled the beans."

Mr. Marcus was Cathy's algebra teacher. She clutched at her throat. "Oh, no. Pray for me."

She found her parents in the den. They turned when she entered: her father, a broad, barrel-chested man still in his golf shoes and Arnold Palmer T-shirt (he usually changed as soon as he got home), her mother looking her usual, slightly disheveled self in a pair of jeans and a paint-speckled blouse. Sybil Meyers was not very concerned about her appearance, maintaining that many other things were more important than how a person looked.

"Well, sit down, Cathleen."

Whenever they called her Cathleen, she knew she was in for it. She lowered herself into a deep leather arm chair.

"We want to talk about your report card," her father said. "Mr. Marcus informed me that you received a D in algebra."

Cathy swallowed hard, her voice sticking in her throat. "Yes."

"I hope this isn't an indication of your other grades, young lady."

"It isn't." She hadn't received a bad grade in anything else, although her father would probably criticize her for dropping from a B to a B minus in American history.

"I hope for your sake, that this time you're telling the truth. You must realize that lying certainly hasn't helped so far."

"Cathy," her mother explained patiently, "we've been very understanding until now, and we haven't interfered with your social life at all. But you're a very bright girl. There's no reason why you should be so close to failing a subject. If you can't buckle down by yourself, we're going to have to help you. For starters, we've hired you a tutor."

Cathy's mouth dropped open. "A tutor?" Gripping the arms of the chair, she asked, "Who?"

"John Crowley, a boy in one of my classes," said Mr. Meyers. "Do you know him?"

"No. Well, maybe. I might've seen him around. Isn't he kind of a creep?" It wasn't the right thing to say to her parents, she knew, but she also knew the sort of person they would choose. It was true she couldn't quite place John Crowley, but she had a vague idea of who he might be—tall, dark-haired, with glasses—one out of a small group of studious, silent types who would view her from the pedestal of the Honor Roll as if she were a real dummy for needing a tutor.

"He isn't a creep, Cathy. He's a very responsible young man, and I think he can help you." Stephen Meyers' explanation was firm.

"I don't want his help, Dad. I don't care what you think of him. I don't want a tutor." Cathy crossed her arms angrily, trying to think of some way out of this whole mess. How embarrassing—having a nerd tutor her in algebra! "Look, I'll study harder, I promise, and I'll get Derek or Jan to help me."

"Cathy, you've made promises before. Besides, you know you wouldn't get much studying done if one of your friends tried to help you. What you need is someone totally uninvolved."

Fidgeting, Cathy jumped to her feet. "Can I go now? I've got to get ready."

Her mother's eyebrows shot up. "Oh? And where are you going?"

"I'm going to Lisa Shuler's party, Mom. I told you that a week ago, remember?"

"Call Lisa and tell her you're not going. And don't make any more plans for the weekend, Cathy," her father said firmly. "Officially, as of now, you're grounded."

"Daddy!"

"We're serious, Cathy."

Her mother looked at her husband, then back at Cathy. "I'm sorry, Cathy, you have to learn. A few weeks' work with John will help you, I'm sure. You've got to concentrate on your studies more."

"Thanks for ruining my whole life!" Cathy turned and ran out of the den. She was ready to explode. Be tutored by John Crowley? What did her parents think they'd accomplish by sticking her with him?

And tonight, of all nights, she was grounded. They had no right to do this, she fumed, thinking of all the good things she wouldn't be allowed to do now—Lisa's party, skating tomorrow, and whatever else the gang came up with.

Suddenly the four walls of Cathy's bedroom seemed to press in on her like a cell.

Chapter Two

"I forgot to ask if you're allowed visitors." Jan stood on Cathy's doorstep, dressed in cream slacks and a bright orange blouse, a begonia pinned in her curly ginger-colored hair.

Tracy walked up the stone path behind her friend.

"Yes, I'm allowed visitors. Come on in." Cathy motioned to them. Horace, the Meyers' red setter, followed the girls in the hope of getting some attention.

Jan seated herself carefully on Cathy's striped bedspread, while Tracy preferred to stand, not wanting to crease her white cotton embroidered dress.

Surveying them both in their party clothes, Cathy said, "I sure wish I was going with you. But I guess I'm stuck here until my algebra gets better—or they invent a new kind of computer for me to swallow."

"Ugh—algebra. It sounds like some kind of

disease, doesn't it?" Tracy wrapped her tongue around the word and tried it out several different ways, until the word sounded funny and foreign to their ears, and they burst into giggles. "Well, anyway, it's a good thing your problem isn't English. You'd really be in the doghouse with your dad."

"Yeah, luckily I've always done well in English without really trying. Dad's only cause for complaint there is that I don't spend my free time curling up with Shakespeare or inventing new uses for the comma."

Jan laughed. "Cathy, you really are too much. So what are they going to do to you?"

Cathy leaned her head back against her rattan headboard. "You mean besides keeping me in solitary confinement? Wait until you hear. You won't believe it. You'd think I was going to be a brain surgeon the way they worry about my math grades. I mean, who needs algebra, right? It's really embarrassing. I can't—"

"Cathy!" Jan interrupted. "Will you just tell us already?"

"They hired someone named John Crowley to tutor me."

"A tutor? What for? That's crazy."

Cathy shrugged. "I don't know why. They just went ahead and hired someone."

"Who's John Crowley, anyway? Does he go to Sierra?"

"Is he cute?" Tracy asked. "I've never heard of him."

Cathy sighed. "I have him pictured as one of those studious types with thick glasses and an armload of books. I'm not sure. He's in one of my dad's classes, though."

"Wouldn't you know it."

"We'll have to check him out." Jan's eyes lit up mischievously.

Cathy knew what that meant. Jan would want to check John's entire class schedule, what he ate for lunch, who he ate with, his daily habits in general. Personally, Cathy thought Jan read too many detective stories and that she applied detective tactics to finding out facts about interesting boys. Then, when she talked to them, she could weave the information into her conversation.

Cathy's strategy was different, however. When she wanted to get a boy to notice her, which she never found difficult, she simply flirted with him. She seemed to have a knack for figuring boys out, for tuning in to their personalities. In this case, though, she wasn't going to bother. She wasn't interested in getting John Crowley to notice her. They would get to know each other soon enough, and, anyway, she was already certain he wasn't her type.

Her type was a popular, outgoing boy, who liked to go to parties and football games, and, above all, liked to dance. Cathy dated regularly but so far, had never fallen for any-one. She thought it was sort of scary to get that involved with a boy. She had seen what happened to her friends when they fell in love—they couldn't concentrate on anything else, and they were crushed if things didn't work out. She was certain she wasn't ready to go through that yet, if ever. She never wanted to lose control over a relationship the way she had seen other girls do, or be inseparable from a boy. At least this way, Cathy knew she wouldn't be the one to get hurt.

Tracy's deep voice cut into her thoughts. "I'm glad my folks aren't teachers. I'm sorry, Cath."

"Don't apologize. I understand. Believe me, I often wish they weren't teachers, either."

"If only you could think of a way to get them off your case." Jan sighed.

"You mean like a brain transplant?" asked Cathy.

"Oh, come on, Cathy," said Tracy. "We know you're no dummy. Just look at all the things you know how to do." She looked around

Cathy's room. "You can skate, you're a good photographer, you can dance—lots of things." She glanced at her watch. "Uh-oh, it's getting late. Sorry, Cath, we've got to go. Anybody you want us to kiss for you?"

Cathy stuck out her tongue. "Get out of here, will you? Kiss them all for me." She laughed, making a grand gesture with her arms.

"Oh, by the way," said Jan, "when is J.C.'s first tutoring session?"

It took Cathy a moment to figure out who Jan was talking about. She was always calling people by their initials. "Oh, you mean John Crowley. I don't know when he's coming."

"Good luck, anyway," Jan said, walking out of the bedroom.

"Thanks, I'll need it," Cathy said, following her friends down the hallway. At that moment Matt roared into the driveway on his go-cart.

"See you!" Cathy shouted above the din. "And have a good time for me."

Chapter Three

At school on Monday Cathy looked around for John Crowley but didn't see him. She wasn't really sure she knew what he looked like, but she thought it would be nice to find out so that she didn't have such an unformed image of him in her mind.

During lunch, conversation consisted entirely of what had happened at Lisa Shuler's party.

"I couldn't believe it," Jan was saying. "Rob McKay and Tracy danced together *all night*. And God only knows what happened when he took her home."

Tracy jabbed Jan in the ribs with her elbow. Tracy was the only one of the three whose embarrassment didn't show itself like a red banner. "Cut it out, Jan," she warned. "Nothing happened after we left. We just"—her eyes grew misty—"kissed."

"Oooh. When are you going to see him again?"

Picking a piece of lint off her slacks, Tracy pretended to be casual. "Oh, probably in biology this afternoon."

They all started laughing.

"And what about you, Jan?" Tracy taunted. "You sure spent enough time talking to Eddie Harrington, in the dark corner next to the stereo."

"We were talking about records, Tracy." Jan made a big deal of pushing a comb through her curly, obstinate hair.

"Wendy and Phil got into a huge argument, as usual. Lisa had to ask them to leave."

"Why'd she do that? They always put on a good show." Cathy grinned, imagining the couple at each other's throats. If ever there were two natural-born actors, they were Wendy and Phil. They couldn't go out for a hot dog without creating a big scene, but to everyone watching, it was kind of entertaining.

Cathy admired people who could scream their heads off in public and get everything off their chests, then feel great afterward. Her parents were the sort who didn't argue much at all, believing that most disputes could be solved by discussion. But Cathy thought they dismissed too many things just for the sake of keeping peace. They enjoyed silence and protected it at any cost, even if they had to ignore problems to do so. If either she or Matt blew up at home, they were always met with their parents' combined wall of frigid disapproval.

"I found out that J.C. is in the one and only fourth year Spanish class," said Jan, her mouth full.

"What? What's that got to do with anything?"

"Well, you know he's a real brain if he's in fourth year Spanish, Cath. There are only about eight kids in the class. You have to pass first, second, and third year to get into it. They're reading stuff like *Don Quixote*."

"I just wonder what I can do to spice up the tutoring. I mean, algebra is so deadly dull. Even writing the numbers in different-colored ink isn't going to do much for it."

"Who knows? John might be a nice guy, even if he's out of it," suggested Tracy.

"I don't know. Maybe I can tell jokes or something."

The thought of spending an hour bent over an algebra text with a boring boy at her side was enough to make Cathy start squirming.

After school Cathy went home and fixed herself some chocolate milk and cookies. It was ten to four, and her mother would be home soon, and shortly after that, John would arrive. She laid her report card on the kitchen table. It was dogeared, because she'd been nervously twisting the corners between her thumb and forefinger all day.

At that moment her mother's station wagon drove into the garage. Cathy went to her room to brush her hair. The doorbell rang, and she hurried to answer it, thinking that her mom had forgotten her key.

"Uh, hello. I'm John Crowley. Is this the Meyers residence?"

The tall, lanky boy on the doorstep shifted the stack of books from one arm to the other before stepping inside. Cathy was startled. He was handsome! He had dark hair, cut shorter than most of the boys she knew, a long, slender nose, and a strong, angular jaw. He did wear glasses, as she had guessed, but they seemed to set off his dark brown, almond-shaped eyes.

Cathy's first thought was: why haven't I noticed this guy before?

Slightly thrown off guard because her idea of what he would look like had been so wrong, she needed a moment to gather her composure enough to speak—which was unusual for her.

"Oh, hi. I'm Cathy, the resident math genius. Come on in."

The click of her mother's low-heeled, sensible shoes sounded across the linoleum. "Oh, hello, John. I see you've already met our Cathy."

"Our Cathy." Cathy's ears burned at the pet phrase. Her mother's fingers touched her elbow, and her smile, expressly meant for John, was that of a person who has just met a comrade after days of battling with some enemy. John was on the side of the teachers, while Cathy was definitely in the league of incorrigible students.

"I was about to make some lemonade. Would you like some, John?" Sybil Meyers asked.

"Uh, yes. That would be nice, thank you," John replied formally.

Cathy drew in her breath. Lemonade, how cute. John seemed so stilted yet so gorgeous. She sneaked another look into those big brown eyes and wondered what he'd look like without his glasses.

"I think the study would be the best place for you two to work, don't you, Cathy?" Sybil said as the frozen lemonade plopped into a plastic pitcher. "There's a nice desk in there and lots of light."

"Or outside," suggested Cathy. "Do you ever do your homework outside, John? I always find that fresh air really gears up my brain. How about you?"

He replied very seriously, "No, I don't. I usually study in my room."

"How original," Cathy muttered under her breath.

Cathy's mother placed two tall glasses on a tray. "Here you go. And here are some cookies Matt made last night."

"Sugar cookies—my favorite," John commented, following Cathy and the tray into the den.

Sugar cookies and lemonade. This boy is just *too, too* far out for me, Cathy thought. Well, she considered, he surprised me once, maybe can surprise me again. And *he is definitely good looking.*

She placed the tray on her father's desk. "This is the place," she announced.

"Your mother was right. This is a good place to work, don't you think?"

Mom is just going to love this guy, I can tell, thought Cathy, as she watched him sit down stiffly in one of the leather chairs.

"Terrific!" Cathy agreed, with mock enthusiasm, but John didn't seem to notice he was being teased. "Well, what do we do first? she asked him.

"Well, why don't you tell me what you're having trouble with, and maybe we can work on it."

Right down to business. At least he could have asked her what her favorite subject was. She wondered if he was aware that he was staring at her peach-painted toenails.

John cleared his throat nervously. "Maybe you could show me your homework and your algebra book?"

"Oh, sure. Just a sec." Cathy skipped off to her room and brought the textbook to him. "Here. Pages two twenty-one through two twenty-four. That's what we're working on now."

Casually perched on the wide arm of his chair, Cathy leaned slightly over him as he read. She was sure her closeness bugged him, so it didn't surprise her when he suggested, a little stiffly, "Shouldn't you find your own chair?"

"Oh, yeah. Sure." Quickly she spun around and flopped into the chair directly across from him, where she could watch him better.

"Where did you start having trouble with algebra, Cathy?" John inquired evenly.

"In Mr. Marcus's class, the very first day." It was the sort of Goldie Hawn answer she was famous for. She studied John's impressive profile to see how he would react. He didn't. What did it take to loosen somebody like him up? she wondered. "I've never been very good at math, but algebra is just impossible for me."

"Do you understand sets and subsets?" he asked, flipping through the book.

She shrugged. "It kind of goes in one ear and out the other. They're so uninteresting they don't stick."

"Uninteresting? I think math is really challenging."

She stared at him as if he had a screw loose, and she wondered whether he was putting her on. There was the slightest twinkle in his eye—or was it just the reflection off his glasses?

John went on. "But I think I understand your problem. A lot of girls are afraid of math. I think it's the way they're brought up. They think they're not supposed to be interested in stuff like that. And it's too bad, because there's no reason why girls can't do as well as boys in algebra, or anything else, for that matter. I—"

"Wait a minute!" Cathy interrupted. "Me?

Afraid? Are you kidding? Listen carefully, John," she said slowly, as if explaining something to a child, "the reason I hate math is because *math is boring!* Besides, I happen to have better things to do with my time than play around with sets and subsets. And another thing, I am not 'a lot of girls.' I'm me. Okay?"

But John kept right on talking, as if he hadn't heard a word she'd said. "Anyway, math just might come in handy someday when you're looking for a job. A lot of people are finding they need to go back to school and take calculus and trig in order to get promotions."

"Well, I don't think that applies to me." Cathy let out a sigh and tossed her hair over her shoulders.

"Why not? What are your plans for the future?"

"Plans? What plans? I'm only sixteen, you know. I don't have to have my future all mapped out already." The question made her a little uneasy, though, so she fired it back at John. "All right, Mr. Mathematics, what do *you* want to do?"

"I want to be a doctor," he told her simply.

I should have known, she thought. Why does he always have to have an an answer for everything? "Well, I've still got a lot of time to decide what I'm going to do. And meanwhile, I just want to have fun."

"Well, you seem like a smart girl. You can be or do anything you want, you know, if you take things seriously."

Cathy glared at him, remembering her parents' concern and the way they kept telling her she had to be more serious about studying if she wanted to go to college. She was sure she had plenty of time to decide about college and plenty of time to get her grades up if she had to. But John's certainty seemed to underline what her parents had told her and to increase her own insecurity. "Gee, John," she said teasingly, "that's the most romantic thing any boy has ever said to me. I hope you don't say that to all the girls."

He changed the subject abruptly. "So, let me see you work some of these problems," he said, handing her the algebra book. "Then I can get an idea of what you can do."

Cathy scanned the page, her brain closing up shop at the sight of the equations she'd never really looked at. "I can't do any of these without help," she admitted.

John bent over the algebra book and launched into a long, detailed explanation of sets of integers, but Cathy lost his drift entirely. Instead, she stared at his square-nailed fingers and at the golden hairs on the back of his hands that glistened under the lamplight as he moved. She also liked how his hair curved neatly against his neck and had a slight wave to it.

"Do you understand?"

When John looked expectantly at her, all she could do was shake her head. "John, don't you ever smile?"

"Of course I do." He managed a quick, self-conscious smile, just to prove to her he had the ability. "When there's something to smile about. You brought your homework, too, right?"

"Yes. Here." She yanked a mimeographed sheet from the book.

"Okay." Again, John explained each problem patiently, looking to Cathy for the answers.

If he had asked her for a description of his hands or the way he held a pencil, she could have given it readily. As it was, all she could do was smile and make wisecracks. "Do you get paid by the hour or by the problem?" she asked.

"Cathy, will you cut out the jokes and pay attention?" His patience was starting to wither. "Now did you see how I got that?"

"I saw it all right, but I sure didn't understand it."

He explained once more how he had arrived at the answer.

At last John and Cathy were finished, the homework done, ready to turn in to Mr. Marcus the next day. While Cathy slipped her homework paper back in her book, her fingers accidentally—or slightly on purpose—touched John's, and he drew back quickly, as if he'd touched fire.

Cathy stole a glance at him and noted that his color had risen to the roots of his dark hair. Ah-hah! she thought. He's not just a human computer after all.

"I guess I'll see you tomorrow," John said as they walked to the front door.

"Okay." Cathy leaned against the doorjamb and watched him walk down the path to his bike.

On impulse, she yelled out, "John!"

He turned in surprise, nearly losing his footing.

"Smile!" She smiled Cheshire cat-style—something she'd practiced in the mirror so often she knew how to do it without looking.

John stared at her with an expression that was half laugh and half grimace, but then, he managed a brief smile as he hopped on his bike and waved goodbye.

Well, what had happened? Cathy had planned to be bored, not interested. Math still wasn't interesting, but John was. She had expected him to be ordinary looking, but he was sensational looking, even if he didn't have any idea he was.

And, he certainly wasn't like any of the other boys Cathy knew—which left her pleasantly confused.

Chapter Four

"What's he like?"

Cathy shrugged as she twisted Jan's hair onto an electric roller. "He's good looking, believe it or not. I sure was surprised when I saw him on the doorstep. Only trouble is, he's fascinated by math."

"That's not all bad." Tracy sat on the edge of the bathtub, watching. "Maybe he'll be a famous scientist someday. Is he interested in sports or anything like that?"

"I don't know. He doesn't say much about himself. We just talked about algebra. He did say he wants to be a doctor."

"We just asked what he did for fun," Jan said, "not what his life's ambitions are."

"How am I supposed to know?" Cathy giggled. "He's strictly business, Jan."

"Who does he hang around with?" Tracy wanted to know.

"I don't know. Hold still, Jan." Cathy

pushed in a thick bobby pin to secure one of the curlers. "Boy, your hair has a mind of its own."

"That's what it keeps telling me," wailed Jan, and they all laughed.

"Can't you just imagine Derek or Tom Williams tutoring you? Or Tim Bryant?" Jan rolled her eyes. "You'd never get any work done, Cathy. No wonder your parents chose J.C. I know those guys are really smart, but their brains never get in the way of having a good time."

"Yeah. *They're* all good students, and *they* still manage to play sports and go to parties," Cathy said thoughtfully. "I guess they don't make a steady diet of studying. I mean, John just seems so—serious. The guy hardly ever smiles."

"That's really something," Tracy marveled. She took an apothecary jar full of polished stones from the shelf and picked through them. "You get smiles out of a boy pretty easily, Cathy. Ms. Personality Plus, that's you. You know so much about boys you could write one of those advice columns in the newspaper. I'm sure your advice would be better than theirs. Hey, maybe you'll be a world-famous psychologist some day."

"I'd rather be a world-famous actress. That would be a lot more fun," Cathy said dramatically.

"How about the first woman president?" Jan suggested. "I can just see you out on the campaign trail."

"Listen to you guys," Cathy complained. "Even you're bugging me about my future now. Why can't anyone just let me enjoy being sixteen for awhile? Anyway, getting back to John, he did smile a little, but I just don't think there's any chemistry between us." Then she remembered that second when their fingers had touched. But she didn't mention it to her friends. She squirted some setting lotion on Jan's hair and mopped up the drips that ran down her neck. "I wonder if he's got a girlfriend."

"He's a senior, isn't he?"

"Yeah, I think so."

"Marcia Hutton. She's been nominated valedictorian." supplied Tracy. "She sounds like his type."

Cathy visualized Marcia's pert, owlish face next to John's and tried to imagine the two holding hands or dancing, but the image seemed cartoonish. "No. They'd both be too embarrassed to fall for each other."

"Marcia's nice, but she's in love with Shakespeare," Tracy said. Marcia was the only girl in Sierra Heights who could give a believable portrayal of Ophelia. She really got into her part.

Jan squealed. "Can't you just imagine kissing a guy who talked in prose like that?"

"Sort of like Cyrano de Bergerac," dreamed Tracy.

"What difference does it make how the guy talks when you're kissing him, Jan?" Cathy demanded.

Tracy started laughing so hard that she slid from the edge of the tub to the fluffy pink bath rug. "You are crazy!" she sputtered.

"I recall having very little to say to Jack Engel when we were going out," Cathy said, unplugging the rollers. "He kissed so well, words would've been a waste of time."

"He still does kiss well, I hear," maintained Jan. "His lips will soon be world famous. By the way, Tim Bryant asked me about you, Cath. Look what you're missing, holed up here at home."

"Tim Bryant had arrived at Sierra in the fall as a new student and had received a lot of attention from the female population there already. "What did Tim say?" Cathy asked.

She had known for several weeks that he'd been eyeing her.

"He asked me if you were dating anyone, and I said no. I told him you were grounded, and he just said, 'Oh.' He sounded disappointed."

"How can you tell he was disappointed from just an 'oh'?" Cathy was skeptical. "Are you sure you're not reading more into the conversation than really exists?"

Jan shook her head. "I know a disappointed boy when I see one."

"He's awfully cute, Cathy," Tracy cooed.

"How long are you grounded for, Cath?" asked Jan.

"Until I get a good grade on my next algebra test. I have to show signs of improvement."

"Let's see how no parties, no dances, no boys affects you," Jan directed a painted fingernail at her. With hairpins protruding at odd angles from her rollers, Jan looked like a Martian. "You'll be itching to get loose in another week."

"Yeah, you're probably right." Cathy rose and slipped on her thongs. She thought of John's dark brown eyes, so full of concentration while he patiently explained problems to her. She pictured him masterfully juggling numbers and tossing them to her, except that she kept fumbling with them and dropping them all over the floor.

Could she ever learn anything from him? She could never learn to concentrate the way he did, but she at least had to get through this semester. With boys, social stuff, and most of her schoolwork, Cathy was pretty sure of herself. But now, with algebra—and John Crowley—a flutter of doubt crept in where only self-confidence had been. Quickly Cathy brushed those disquieting thoughts aside. One hour five days a week with John was bound to make a difference.

She turned to Jan. "Come on. Let's go outside and watch your hair curl."

"John's coming after dinner tonight," Cathy announced at dinner, having just talked to him briefly on the phone.

It was a disappointing conversation. He was Mr. Business and had only said what he needed to say, nothing more. Cathy didn't really know why she felt he should have said more, especially since he'd be at her home right after dinner but still, the conversation seemed too abrupt.

"John is such a nice boy, isn't he?" Sybil Meyers said as she spooned peas onto her husband's plate. "Don't you like him, Cathy?"

She glared at the bold brown line around the edge of her stoneware plate. "I guess so. I hardly know him. One tutoring session does not a friendship make, Mother."

"His father suffered a back injury recently, you know. He's recuperating from surgery now. I suppose John's trying to earn some extra money for the family."

"No, I didn't know," Cathy said. "John didn't mention his family."

"Did you do better on your homework, Cathy?" her father asked.

Cathy rolled her eyes and motioned that her mouth was full.

"Wait," Matt interjected on her behalf. "Can't you see the poor girl's masticating her food?"

"Is that one of your vocabulary words for this week?" Stephen Meyers inquired with amusement.

"It's a bonus word, Dad. I've got to think up sentences for all of them," Matt explained.

Cathy cleared her throat noisily to get their attention. "If anyone's still interested, I didn't get my homework back yet, but John did help me with it, and, yes, I think I did better."

"Bravo." Her father smiled. "Mr. Marcus ought to be happy about that."

John was wearing a light blue pinstriped shirt with dark blue cords, which looked nice on him, Cathy thought. Except that John never looked casual. Other boys could somehow make the same combination look casual, but not John.

Cathy sat across from him on a cushioned rattan chair.

"I never see you around school, John. Do you spend a lot of time at the library counting the books?" Cathy propped her chin in her palm and waited expectantly for his answer. She had put on green eyeshadow and new mascara, hoping he would notice that something was different about her.

"Sometimes."

She winked. "You sound so mysterious. Do you play sports or anything?"

"No, I don't." Looking uncomfortable, he crossed and recrossed his ankles, then opened a book in his lap. "I do play chess."

"I'm glad to hear you play something." She couldn't resist a smile.

His blush rose from his collar. "Let's do some algebra, Cathy."

"Okay, okay," Cathy agreed. "I just didn't want to jump right into it, you know? My heart can't take so much excitement all at once. You're my only contact with the outside world, and I've got to make the most of it, you know. I'm grounded until I get a decent grade on the next algebra test. Did my folks tell you?"

He shook his head.

"We have them every two weeks, so I'm hoping to up my score on the next one."

"I think it might help if you changed your attitude a little."

"It sounds like *you've* been taking lessons from my parents. You have this funny way of sounding *exactly* like them. Look, I can have fun and still get by. I've done it all through school . . . Besides, you're going to help me."

"I can't pass algebra for you, Cathy. You've got to do some of the work yourself. Don't think I'm going to save you."

"Thanks a lot. It's nice to know my tutor has so much confidence in me."

John sighed. "Why don't we just cut out the personal stuff and get down to work, okay?"

"It's okay with me. Go ahead, Professor Crowley, sir."

". . . Apply the distributive law and re-write each collection of symbols without parentheses as illustrated in the examples."

He handed her a freshly sharpened pencil.

Cathy accepted the pencil daintily. "Why, thank you." After dinner, she had changed into a sleeveless white T-shirt that showed off the beginning of a tan. Now, she was getting cold and excused herself to get a sweater.

When Cathy returned, John looked annoyed, but he didn't say anything. She concentrated for a few minutes on one problem, then said softly, "I need your help, John. I can't do this."

Seeming reluctant, he moved closer to her to help. "Look, all you have to do is add five plus two, then multiply by three."

Slowly, Cathy worked several problems. And John stayed next to her the whole time.

"There!" She finally sat back and handed him her work.

He studied the sheet carefully. "This one is good, Cathy, but the others are wrong."

Cathy frowned at him. "What do you mean, wrong? I did what you said!"

"Well, let's go back over them." Patiently, he showed her what she had done wrong. Then together they arrived at the correct answer.

"How exciting," said Cathy under her breath, not without sarcasm.

"You're doing great," John said, consulting

his watch, which let her know there wasn't much time left.

She was amazed at how good those few words of praise from him made her feel. "You really think so?"

"Sure."

Cathy stared at him, noting how his eyebrows were hidden by the tortoise-shell rim of his glasses.

"You know, John," she said teasingly, "most girls would probably want you to take off your glasses, but *I* think you look terrific with them on."

"Oh, I guess you don't want to see me turn into Superman, then, huh?" John said with a straight face.

She laughed. "You're funny, John. Did you know that?"

He stacked up his books, ready to leave. "No one has ever called me funny before, Cathy. I'm not a funny person."

"Maybe you are, and just don't know it. I think you have a hidden fantastic sense of humor," Cathy ventured, "Who are your friends? Maybe their funniness has rubbed off on you," she joked, but it was also a sly way of getting information.

"Do you know Paul Eisley and Jud Donnalan?" he asked, placing his pencil in his shirt pocket.

"No."

"Those are my friends," he told her, the corners of his mouth tilting slightly upward with only the hint of a smile. "And now, I've got to go. See you tomorrow."

"'Bye."

After he was gone, Cathy lingered in the study, thinking: Wow, he's even got a sense of humor buried deep down under all those equations. John Crowley is certainly full of surprises.

Chapter Five

When Cathy arrived at school the next morning, there was a noisy commotion in the hallway, and she couldn't get to her locker.

"What's up?" she asked Lisa Shuler, who was craning her neck to see over a sea of heads.

"Somebody put a bra over the George Washington bust in the display cabinet," Lisa informed her.

"You're kidding. Do they know who?" Cathy, being short, had to stand on tiptoes to catch a glimpse of Ms. Fisher, guidance counselor, extracting the bra from the cabinet, getting the strap hooked on Washington's nose en route.

"Of course not. It was probably some freshman, though. Who else would do such an immature thing?"

Cathy laughed. Lisa behaved as though immaturity was a sin, she thought, stopping at her locker, then hurrying to her algebra class.

Mr. Marcus, Cathy's algebra teacher, was a good friend of her father's, and close to the same age. He looked older to Cathy, though, with stripes of gray hair on either side of his head. Ever since he told her father about her grade in his class, she had considered him to be against her. She behaved all right in class—well, maybe she talked a little more than she should. But even when she was quiet, Mr. Marcus always managed to look at her with a slight air of disapproval, which really bothered her.

Now she passed her homework paper forward, feeling relief that she'd done the work and knowing that it was probably correct, too. What would she do without John? Actually, he'd done most of the work. She smiled to herself, thinking about how cute he looked when he was concentrating.

On the inside cover of her notebook, Cathy absentmindedly wrote the names Paul Eisley and Jud Donnalan, then doodled around the two names. Those were John's friends. What were they like? Were they as serious as he was? Even she had to admit, her experience with this type of boy was limited—she who could attract nearly any boy she wanted.

Cathy clapped a cold palm to her cheek, as if trying to bring herself to her senses. What was she thinking? Why should she be concerned with attracting John, anyway? He was—well, he was a challenge, that's what he was, and sort of a mystery, too. Besides, he really was good looking. But she certainly didn't want to get serious about him. It was just fun imagining the possibilities. If she ever got to know John and he liked her back, the excitement would fizzle out of their relationship like carbonation out of an open soft drink, just the way it had with all the other boys.

When the bell rang, Cathy jumped out of her seat and made a dash for the door. Often her dad would come to Mr. Marcus' room after first period to talk, and she didn't want to run into him today.

"Hey, Cath." Derek Sorenson clapped her on the back, tipping her slightly forward.

"Derek, you have the heaviest hands of anybody I know!" Cathy exclaimed, recovering herself.

"Oh, sorry, I forgot. I don't know my own strength." He looked bashful. "I wanted to know if you wanna go rafting this weekend? Marty's taking us out again this Saturday."

Her parents' restriction tightened invisibly around her. "Oh, you know I'd love to, Derek, but I'm grounded. Didn't you know? I'm pretty sure I can't go."

He shook his head in dismay. "Too bad. Love to have you aboard, you know. Can't you talk 'em out of it?" His face was hopeful.

"No. It's because of my math grade. I have to bring up my algebra before they'll let me off," she explained.

"Well, I'll be thinking of you as we race over that white water." He grinned.

"I'll be thinking of you, too." Ahead, Cathy spotted John standing in a triangle of sunlight at the end of the hall. It was the first time she'd seen him at school. "See you, Derek," she said absently, hurrying toward John.

He was talking to two boys she didn't know.

"John!" she called, waving to him.

His head jerked up. The sound of her voice had obviously startled him. "Oh—uh—Cathy, hello. How are you?" You couldn't exactly say John sounded pleasantly surprised, but that didn't stop Cathy.

"Oh, you know me, John, laughing on the outside, crying on the inside, as usual. Hey, do you realize this is the first time we've ever met in public?"

"Yeah, well, I guess it is." He looked like a trapped animal desperate for escape. Cathy noticed the other two boys eyeing her with curiosity and interest. But John made no move to introduce them. In fact, he seemed to be trying hard to pretend that the whole episode wasn't happening. But Cathy plunged ahead. "So, these must be the friends you were telling me about." She turned to a freckle-faced boy of about her own height. "Hi, I'm Cathy Meyers."

"Oh, yeah, Mr. Meyers' daughter, aren't you?"

She sighed and flipped her hair over her shoulder. "Why is it I'm only recognized as 'Mr. Meyers' daughter'? What if he was Cathy Meyers' father? How would that be?"

The boy blushed, making his freckles all the more prominent. "Sorry. I didn't mean to offend you."

"Oh, no big deal," Cathy said.

"I'm Jud Donnalan, by the way," the boy said.

Cathy grinned. "Nice to meet you, and nice of John to forget to introduce us." She shot a half-smile John's way.

The other boy chuckled and looked at John.

John cleared his throat. "Well, Cathy—" he

began, but she cut him off, turning her attention to the other boy.

"And you must be Paul." Cathy smiled. Paul, a milky-skinned, towheaded boy, nodded and said hi.

"Well, listen, would you like to go out for a Coke after school, instead of meeting at my house, the way we usually do?" she suggested, looking directly into his dark eyes. Jud and Paul were getting more and more curious, but Cathy didn't notice them. A thrill passed through her as, for once, John looked right back into her eyes and gave her his full attention. But it only lasted a second, and then he was backing away again.

"Look, Cathy, my next class is in there, and I'm going to be late, and so are you." He nodded toward one of the art rooms.

She was vaguely aware of Paul and Jud shuffling into class. By John's body language, she could tell that he more than half wanted to be in his classroom. In fact, about three-quarters of him wanted to be sitting in front of that teacher, and only one-quarter wanted to talk to her.

"Well, do you want to?" Cathy persisted, clutching her binder demurely against her chest, following him to the door. He was looking intently at her again. Then the bell rang above them, making John jump. But Cathy stood her ground.

"Look, I can't . . . I'm sorry. I'll see you later . . . 'Bye. I'm late." He was gone.

Unbelievable, Cathy thought, as she trudged down the stairs. Any other boy would have been happy with her invitation—but not John.

That evening, when he came to tutor her, Cathy said casually, "I guess you had something to do after school today?"

"My father asked me to come straight home from school," he replied, not looking up from the algebra homework he was correcting.

"Oh, are you in trouble?" In Cathy's book, having your dad summon you straight home from school meant trouble.

"No, nothing like that. He just needed me to drive him somewhere."

From the closed look on John's face, Cathy knew it was the end of that conversation.

What bugged her was why he didn't take a rain check on her offer. Why did he say absolutely nothing about it? Was he just too shy or embarrassed?

It might be the end of the conversation, Cathy decided, but it was only the beginning of the J.C. Mystery.

Chapter Six

"You got a B on an algebra test. Cathy, you've really made some progress!" Stephen Meyers praised his daughter. He lay the test paper on the coffee table. "John must be just the right tutor for you."

She shrugged. It annoyed her how her parents wanted to take credit for everything. They chose John, therefore they were the ones responsible for her good grade. "He helps," she replied. "He's madly in love with numbers, and he's trying to make me see how wonderful they are, too. Have I got news for him."

"John's a nice boy, don't you think?" Sybil smoothed the Indian print skirt she wore, which looked to Cathy like a garage sale find. Knowing her mother, it probably was.

"Sure, he's nice. Kind of boring, though."

"That's unfair, Cathy. And you know what John must be going through with his family right now." Sybil Meyers frowned disapprovingly.

"I don't know anything about him, Mom. He never talks about himself to me."

It was completely true. In the two weeks she'd been working with John, as much as she had tried to unearth something about his personal life, they had never talked about him, only about algebra. Cathy suspected that he was inclined to confide more in her parents than in her, which for some reason made her slightly jealous. They were just parents, for crying out loud, not friends.

She had tried to draw him out, flirting with him a little, and more than once she had detected a flicker of interest on that intelligent, watchful face. But then, he always seemed to back away. She couldn't figure him out. Oh, well, at least she hadn't lost her touch with other boys.

"Since I'm doing so well with my algebra, can I go out tomorrow night, maybe?" Cathy asked casually. Tim Bryant had asked her to go with him to a dance at the school. She had waited to get her parents' permission until she had got her algebra test score. Now she held her breath, praying they'd say yes.

"Oh, dear. I don't know." Sybil Meyers looked to her husband for a reply.

Cathy's father sucked thoughtfully on his pipe. "I suppose so. You do deserve a night out, and we did promise we'd lift the restriction if your grade improved. But—" he adopted a sudden, stern tone— "this doesn't mean we're back to the old fun and games, young lady. No more all play and no work. You're still going to have to work hard on that math, so there will be no going out on school nights."

"Sure, I know. Thanks, Dad." She went to her room to phone Tim.

He was extremely popular, and Jan and Tracy were both drooling when she told them he had asked her out.

"You're looking good, Cathy," Tim complimented her as he held open the door of his orange Karmann Ghia. Tim Bryant was tall with dark, curly hair, and a perfect muscular build.

"Why, thank you, so are you." She smiled and fluttered her eyelashes.

Cathy did look good, with her bangs combed to one side and her hair gently curled at the ends. She had on a red blouse with billowy sleeves and a Hawaiian print skirt—since the theme of the dance was Hawaiian.

Suddenly she started wondering how John would like her outfit. Then she remembered who she was with and nestled closer to Tim.

"Hey, that's nice," he commented.

Cathy looked at him. "You're getting a great tan," she said. "Are you out in a sun a lot?"

"Yeah, pretty much." He shrugged. "I'm pretty athletic."

"You're a center on the basketball team, right?" she cooed.

"Well, yeah. I spend a lot of time inside a gym, too, you know." He turned and winked at her, and she flashed a smile at him.

"That Hawaiian shirt really shows off your tan," Cathy added.

"Oh—thanks," he replied, obviously flattered.

Cathy was glad to see she hadn't lost her touch.

"What were you grounded for, Cathy?" Tim asked as they parked in back of the auditorium where the dance was being held.

"My report card. Algebra, mainly. But I've got a tutor who's helping me." The air was growing chilly, so she slipped on her sweater.

"Why didn't you ask me? I'd tutor you." He grinned at her and slid an arm around her shoulders.

"My parents chose my tutor. He's good. Do you know John Crowley?"

Tim frowned in concentration. "Oh, yeah. I know him. *He's* tutoring you? He's in my trig class."

"Oh, really?"

"Did you know John won a CSF scholarship?" Tim held her hand as they strolled into the auditorium.

"No, I didn't know," Cathy replied, feeling a twinge of jealousy. Why did everyone in the world seem to know more about John than she did? "John never tells me anything."

"I just happened to know because Pete Price got one, too, and he's a close friend of mine." He squeezed her shoulders. "But wouldn't you rather have me? I bet John's kind of dull, isn't he?"

Cathy didn't answer as they passed under the straw arch that was supposed to look like a grass shack but looked more like a lopsided arrangement of hay bales. Fortunately, there wasn't time to dwell on Tim's question, for they were greeted by Tracy and her new interest, Rob McKay. Jan was with Eddie Harrington, and they waved from across the dance floor, then came over.

"Hi, you two." Jan winked at Cathy. "So you got out of the house, huh, Cathy? This is going to be a great dance."

"I hope so. I have to make the most of tonight, since I'm not allowed to go out during the week."

They talked for a few more minutes. Then Tim suggested that he and Cathy head for the refreshment table. Jan took Eddie's hand, and they went off to dance again.

After Tim had sampled everything at the refreshment table, he and Cathy danced. Cathy loved to dance, and she was good at it, having taken lessons for a year and a half. The rhythm got under her skin and moved her almost of its own will, and she flowed with it as if she were going for a ride. When she danced, she came to life, momentarily forgetting everything else, except the music and her partner.

Tim's hazel eyes shone with admiration as he spun her around and around. Cathy's heart rose into her throat as she looked at him. He was so good looking—every girl's dream of an ideal date. And he was a good dancer, too, though she knew he was not her equal.

She wondered if John danced. . . .

Cathy and Tim danced almost every dance and Cathy was sorry when the evening was over. Tim suggested driving along by the river. It was a balmy, romantic night. The headlights blazed a bright path through the darkness. They could see tiny waves glittering by moonlight, and on the horizon, pines merging with a starless, deep purple sky, creating a feeling of immensity that took Cathy's breath away.

At Cathy's house, they sat in the car, talking quietly. Tim draped an arm around Cathy's shoulders, stroking the silky sleeve of her blouse. Then he turned to kiss Cathy good night and drew her eagerly into his arms. Her pulse leaped when his lips touched hers.

The thought stole, unbidden, from the back of her mind: *how would John kiss me?*

And then, Tim's arms tightened around her, and she felt the hard ridges of his rib-cage beneath his shirt, pressed close to her body. John's kisses would be altogether different, Cathy told herself. She imagined herself in his arms instead, running her fingers lightly along the spare contours of his face, memorizing them. . . .

A cricket's monotonous song, woven into the steady gurgle of the distant river, suddenly sounded loud to Cathy, reminding her of the time. Gracefully, she extracted herself from Tim's embrace.

"I'd better go in now," she whispered sweetly.

He grinned and kissed her one last time. "Okay, I wish you didn't have to. But see you Monday, okay?"

"Okay."

Cathy watched Tim's car roar off down the road before she slid the key into the lock and went inside.

Chapter Seven

"Do you like to dance, John?" Cathy leaned back in one of the leather chairs and watched John organize his lesson for the day.

"No, and I don't like loud music, fast cars, or football, either. I'm a total loser as a teenager, Cathy. I've got more important things—"

She was so furious she stopped him in mid-sentence. "Why do you always have to put other people down for having fun? Just because you don't know how to have a good time yourself."

"And why do you always try to embarrass me by asking silly questions when I'm trying to teach you something?"

"Well, maybe there are a few things I could teach *you* if you weren't afraid to learn—like how to dance, for instance."

"Look, Cathy. I'm here to do a job. I'm getting paid to teach you something. Maybe you don't care whether you learn anything, but I hate to take your parents' money for nothing.

Some of us do have to take life a little more seriously than you do, Cathy. Believe me."

She was ready to make another smart remark. But then she took a good look at him. He looked terrible, really exhausted and run-down. Why hadn't she noticed it before? "Listen, why don't we take a quick break, go out for ice cream, and then start all over, okay?" She smiled to show him there were no hard feelings.

John smiled back. "Okay. My treat."

At last, Cathy thought gleefully, he's coming under my spell.

Matt met them in the hallway and was immediately indignant. "Hey, where are you guys going? Knocking off early, I see? Aren't you supposed to study until five?"

"We're taking a break," explained John.

Matt grinned. "I bet I know whose idea this was. My dear sister's, that's whose." He made a face at Cathy.

Cathy returned an equally ugly face. "Just tell Mom we'll be back in a little while."

Away from her house, perhaps John would loosen up a little more, Cathy thought, walking beside him. She hoped so.

"There's an ice cream shop nearby —Sally's," she offered.

"Fine," John said.

"Would you call this a date?" Cathy asked teasingly.

"I call it a mid-afternoon break." He looked down at her, his long strides giving her the feeling that she was running to keep up with him.

"Do you have brothers and sisters?" she asked.

"Two sisters and a brother," he answered.

"I don't know about yours, but my brother drives me crazy."

"Mine's about the same age."

"Oh, yeah?"

"Yeah."

Cathy tried as hard as she could, but she could extract very little information from John. He answered her questions in as few words as possible.

Once inside the pink-and-white-striped ice cream shop, Cathy took an interminably long time to decide that, out of forty flavors, she wanted a vanilla ice cream soda. John rolled his eyes in exasperation.

"All that time to choose something so simple?"

"I could've chosen plain and simple vanilla ice cream," she reminded him, scooping out some of the ice cream with a long spoon.

John folded his hands in front of him on

the clear plastic tabletop. "I want to talk to you."

She grinned. "Go ahead. You want to know all about me, right?"

"No."

The word came out so abruptly, Cathy was taken aback, practically choking on her ice cream.

"I want to talk to you about your most unfavorite subject. You're bright, Cathy, and there's no reason in the world why you can't learn algebra if you want to. But it will take you twice as long if you keep goofing around like this." His dark eyes were so earnest.

"Like what? I thought we needed a break. You agreed." She tried to stop her voice from thinning into a whimper. She hated whimpering girls, and she suspected boys did, too.

"That's not the point, Cathy. You make it hard for me to teach you. You have to get that grade up, and just because you did so well on the last test doesn't mean you can relax now."

My fears exactly, John, she thought, but instead she put on a smile and said, "I'll do just fine, John. With you by my side, how can I go wrong?" Her fingernails grazed his palms, and she wiggled her fingers. "Ticklish?"

He pulled his hands into his lap.

"I bet you are ticklish, aren't you?" she persisted, watching him while she took a sip of her soda. He didn't respond. "You're a very mysterious person, John. I mean, I know next to nothing about you!"

"Mystery is only a fringe benefit," he said darkly. "Algebra is what I'm paid to teach you."

She giggled. "You sound exactly like my father, you know that?"

"Cathy, you're making this difficult for both of us."

"You're beginning to repeat yourself."

"I mean it."

Her anger simmered very close to the surface. "I thought we were going to relax for a minute. But I don't think you're capable of it."

"And I don't think you're capable of being with a boy for five minutes without acting like a ridiculous flirt."

Cathy felt the anger spreading, pushing them apart. "John. . ." her voice was a stunned whisper that he cut off.

"Why am I spending my time trying to teach you what you don't want to learn? I may need the money, but I don't think it's worth it." His once softly expressive eyes now blazed at Cathy, making her wish she were invisible.

Her mouth dropped open, but no words would form. It was obvious that there was nothing she could do or say to alter what was happening. John stormed out of the shop, louvered doors banging behind him, his slender back rigid with anger.

Chapter Eight

Cathy had no more desire for her soda after John walked out, so she left it and shuffled dazedly back home. How could things have gone so wrong? She had really tried to help John relax. Why had he gotten so angry?

When she got home, she looked hopefully for John's old black bike, which he usually propped up against the brick planter at the side of the house. It wasn't there.

Stepping into the cool hallway, Cathy wondered what she should tell her mother and hastily sifted through the possibilities: a) John suddenly had got sick and had gone home; b) John had to get home early today and do something for his mother; or c) the truth—she and John had had a slight (?) disagreement.

"John left." Matt thrust his tousled head out of his room to report. "Just took off like a bullet on that old bike of his."

Cathy scowled. "Did he say anything?" The less said, the better.

"Nope. Not to me. He told Mom he had to get home early today, and not to pay him as much because he didn't put in very much time." Matt studied her closely, as if looking for something that would let him know what had really happened. "What's the matter? Did you have a fight or something?"

A wave of relief swept over Cathy—*Thank you, John, for not spilling the beans.* He had paved the way for her with Mom.

She was suddenly aware of Matt's piercing gaze. "Oh, uh, a fight? No, I don't fight with *John,*" she told him, as if the idea were unheard of.

"I heard you asking him if he danced. Geez, Cathy," Matt wagged his head in disgust.

"Eavesdropper. What do you know at thirteen?" she countered.

He grinned out of one side of his mouth, an oil smudge on his right cheek making him look comical. "You'd be surprised!" He laughed, then sauntered back into his room, which was a veritable pig's sty, in Cathy's opinion. You couldn't enter without breaking an ankle on an electronic game or a mechanical part. The closet doors were emblazoned with decals and flourescent posters of cars and motorbikes; the dresser was covered with models in various stages of construction. For his birthday Cathy had bought him a notice that read: *Enter At Your Own Risk*, which was hung on the door.

Cathy went into her room and gazed out at the garden through her bedroom window. A bluejay hopped on a camellia bush and flitted from branch to branch. The whirlybird sprinkler flung drops against her windows, and she felt a stab of annoyance at her mother for placing the sprinkler too close to her room. Now her mother would make her clean the windows again soon.

Sometimes she could look outside and forget any troubles she might have—which had never been very many. She'd managed to breeze through adolescence without the problems many of her friends had. Good old Cathy, she was never down for long.

But today Cathy could not quiet her troubled and confused thoughts. The events of just forty-five minutes before played over and over again in her mind, and a sick, twisting ache of regret rose from her stomach. In the past she could usually tell in advance how people—especially boys—would react to her teasing. But with John, even when she was trying to be nice, her plans always backfired, and he ended up getting angry.

Restless and unable to study, Cathy tiptoed so nobody would hear her down the hall to the den, where she retrieved her algebra homework. John had left it neatly folded on top of her binder.

A lump rose in her throat as she gazed longingly at the leather chair where John had sat. She thought of his hands pale against the dark leather, his elbows jutting out, his expression serious as he talked about algebra.

Knowing that lump was holding back tears, Cathy quickly scooped up her things and went back to her room. Eager to get her mind off her misery, she dialed Jan's number.

Jan sounded strange, as if she were talking into a handkerchief.

"Are you disguising your voice?" Cathy teased her.

"No, eating a bologna sandwich. I've got to keep my strength up. Mom's threatening to make another casserole tonight, and I just can't swallow another bit of casserole!" she said emphatically. "So, how was old J.C. today?"

"That's what I want to talk to you about. Can you come over?"

"Sure, I'll be right there."

" . . . So he got up and stomped out of the ice cream parlor and just left me sitting there. I couldn't believe it."

"I guess you got him pretty upset," Jan commented. "What did you say, anyway?"

"Nothing, I was really trying to be nice and put him at ease. I just can't figure him out. I mean, you can't carry on a normal, everyday conversation with him like you can with other boys."

Jan glanced sideways at her friend. "Cathy, you never have been known to carry on a normal, everyday conversation with boys. Every word drips with honey—even to guys you don't like."

Cathy frowned. "You make me sound terrible."

"What's so terrible about it? I think you're just naturally flirtatious. Nothing wrong with it, really. Boys love it. You can see the marvelous results."

"Not anymore," Cathy said sadly.

"John's cute, but he's really not your type,

Cath. Take my word for it. Unless old J.C. has already broken your heart," she teased.

The corners of Cathy's mouth twisted against her will, as they did when she knew she was about to cry. "Don't be ridiculous." She tried to laugh, but the laugh emerged false and brittle.

Jan changed the subject. "Hey, are you going out with Tim this weekend?" she asked.

"He hasn't asked me."

"Derek says he's going to," Jan informed her.

Cathy smiled, recalling how Tim had pushed so urgently past other students in order to sit next to her during the assembly today at school; how their shoulders had touched, how he had drummed his fingers against the seat of the folding chair, while she'd wondered if he really wanted to hold her hand. But, for once, she'd had enough of thinking about boys.

"Am I ever hungry," she said.

"Ugh. I'm not in the mood for Monday casserole, I'll tell you that," grumbled Jan.

Cathy laughed. Jan's mother went on wild food binges whenever she bought new appliances or cookbooks. When she'd first purchased a new blender, everything was served pureed. They ate soup and stew for the month after she bought a slow cooker. Now her sister had bought her a casserole cookbook, so Mrs. Mason was still trying out new recipes on the family.

"No such luck," Jan complained grimly. "I hate my food all mushed together. It's like eating baby food. I mean, if I was one hundred years old and had very few teeth, perhaps I'd appreciate what she's doing for me."

"Maybe you can eat at my house," suggested Cathy. "I think it's a pretty safe bet my mom won't be fixing a casserole tonight. I saw some pork chops thawing." There was no telling what her mother would do with those chops, however. She experimented with so many different varieties of food you never knew what you'd be getting: Indian, African, Chinese, Mexican, Polynesian—the list was endless.

"Thanks for the invitation," Jan breathed. "I think you might've just saved my life."

The idea occurred to Cathy that having Jan for dinner would discourage her mother from asking about John.

John's words played back: *Cathy, you're making this difficult for both of us.* Jan had said she couldn't carry on a normal, everyday conversation with a boy without flirting. Was that really true?

It just couldn't be, she decided. Perhaps Jan was more correct in saying that John wasn't her type. *That* she could buy much more easily.

Chapter Nine

On Friday, Cathy took an algebra test, which she knew she did badly on. All week she'd been on edge, unable to concen-trate, anticipating this failure and yet feeling helpless to do anything about it.

John had been no help, either, though he might have thought he was helping. "Are you sure you're ready for this test, Cathy? You've got to do well on this one, you know."

"I'm ready, I'm ready," she assured him, knowing she wasn't. Her mind was a million miles away, and she had grasped at any distraction from math: dawdling over clothes, shoes, and record albums.

And all week she thought about John. He didn't want her to be a flirt. But he *did* like her, she knew that. How could he like her and hate her at the same time?

After the math test, Tim Bryant asked Cathy if she wanted to double date with Rob and Tracy, and she readily accepted. Like a convict preparing to meet the executioner, she wanted to cram in as much fun as possible before the ax fell.

Then at lunch Tracy asked her if she wanted to spend the night afterward. "I bought two new albums," she said.

"Oh, sure. Why not?" Cathy grinned, knowing it would be the last time she'd be allowed to for a while.

Of course, the subject of algebra reared its ugly head before dinner, as she guessed it might.

"How did the test go today, Cathy?" her father inquired from the top of a stepladder. He was replacing a curtain rod.

Her mother was putting up applesauce, and the aroma of simmering apples filled the air. Home seemed extra "homey" tonight, and Cathy suddenly wished she didn't have this burning secret to keep from her parents. It made her feel apart from them, and a little ashamed.

Making an unnecessary amount of noise with the silverware, she finally sang out as casually as she could, "Oh, fine. I think I did well."

"Ed did say you were improving," Stephen Meyers said, descending the ladder.

Who else gets daily progress reports on their children, direct from the teacher? Cathy thought bitterly. Still, Mr. Marcus wouldn't see how badly she'd done on this test until he corrected papers this weekend. Just wait until Monday. . . .

She asked if she could spend the night at Tracy's.

"I suppose so, but you'll have to stay in Sunday to finish all your homework," her father warned.

"Can you do the French bread, Cathy?" Sybil Meyers asked. She was ladling steaming applesauce into mason jars. "I've still got a few more jars to fill here. I guess I'll freeze some apple pies, too."

"Now apple pie sounds fabulous." Cathy's father's eyes lit up, and she was glad to see the conversation moving away from algebra. "That's the most ordinary American thing you've thought of in a long time, Sybil."

Sybil Meyers smiled through steam. "Why, thank you, Stephen," she said, winking.

At first, Cathy was embarrassed to see her mother flirting with her father. Then she decided they should try it more often. She ran upstairs to get ready to go out.

* * *

The foursome chose to see a horror movie, which had Cathy and Tracy clinging to their dates' arms.

After the movie Rob grumbled good-naturedly, "Tracy grabbed me so hard I thought she'd rip my arm right off."

"Look at it this way, McKay. When do you ever get girls to cuddle so close?" said Tim.

"That's right." Cathy laughed. "I was ready to climb into your lap a couple of times."

"Why didn't you? You know I wouldn't have minded," Tim said, reaching for her hand. His touch warmed her, and she glanced up to find him gazing fondly down at her. Then, embarrassed, he looked away.

It wasn't hard to figure out that he liked her a lot. Cathy knew that look—she'd seen it on other boys' faces after she'd dated them a couple of times. Their features softened, and their eyes took on an I'd-do-anything-for-you expression. Girls often asked her, "How'd you do it?" as if she had some secret magic charm. Up until now she hadn't been able to answer that question, for it was something she didn't give much thought to. But then Jan's words spiraled through Cathy's mind. *Every word drips with honey—even to guys you don't like.* She put that unpleasant thought out of her mind, however, as they drove to the Viewpoint.

The Viewpoint was a flat, remote turnout that overlooked the entire town, its sparse lights twinkling below like jewels pressed into black velvet.

The Viewpoint was where girls were asked to go steady, where couples broke up and got back together again, where secrets were shared and promises made and broken. Needless to say, it was a romantic place, enclosed by the comforting presence of dense pines and watched over by a star-encrusted sky.

Tim and Cathy sat in the back seat of Rob's car, kissing, while Rob and Tracy strolled along one of the many trails leading away from the Viewpoint.

Tonight, Tim's kisses became more fervent, traveling over her neck and face, sending chills up Cathy's spine, before she pushed him away. "Why don't we go for a walk?" she suggested, freeing an arm from his embrace to motion toward the trails.

"Oh, Cathy," Tim murmured, stroking her hair, which had picked up the static electricity from his shirt. "I really care about you."

Eyes shining, he leaned over to kiss her again, but Cathy inched across the seat to the door. Suddenly his affection seemed to be hemming her in. The tiny compact car with its fogged-in windows and Tim's breath against her cheek was stifling.

"Come on, Tim. It's a beautiful night. Let's walk," she urged.

"Okay," he agreed, but his voice was edged with disappointment.

Cathy smoothed her hair, feeling slightly nervous. She knew she didn't want to get any further involved with Tim. She knew she didn't want him to kiss her again. And she knew she had to find a way to let him know how she felt . . . and soon.

But she wouldn't do it tonight, Cathy decided, as she and Tim strolled along the wide, tree-canopied footpath together. The night was too beautiful, softly cushioning them in its balmy warmth—too beautiful to spoil with any sadness.

Later, after the boys had let Tracy and Cathy off at Tracy's house, the girls put on a stack of albums while Cathy set Tracy's glossy black hair.

Tracy made hot chocolate and toast, then the two lay in twin beds and talked.

"What do you think of Rob?" Tracy asked over and over again.

"He's cute. You know that. What do you want my opinion for?" Cathy finally answered, getting exasperated. "He seems to be crazy about you. So why worry?" She couldn't understand all this concern.

"Oh, he is not."

"Yes, he is, too. I know when a guy is crazy about a girl," Cathy assured her knowledgeably.

"Then you know Tim's crazy about you, too."

Cathy sighed deeply. "I know. I'm not excited about it, Tracy. You think you've got problems. Tim's a nice boy, there's nothing wrong with him that I can see. It's just . . . I don't want to get involved."

"But *why?* You're a cute couple." Tracy propped herself on one elbow to stare at her friend in amazement. "How can you be so unexcited? Haven't you ever felt really special about someone, Cathy?"

"No. I never wanted to, either."

"Do you like playing hard-to-get, is that it?" Tracy pursued. "I noticed you sort of doing that to Tim."

A thin thread of fear wove through Cathy's thoughts as Tracy tried to pinpoint her behavior with Tim. She laughed. "Hard to get?

No, I just had to cool him off, Tracy," she explained quickly. "Actually, I don't *play* hard-to-get, I *am* hard to get."

Tracy laughed. "I guess that's what keeps boys crazy about you. Does John have a crush on you, too?"

"I don't think so. He's in love with subsets and integers. He's really much too serious for me," she said.

"Cathy?"

"What?"

"I know you like him," Tracy said softly, her smile shining through the darkness.

"Ha ha," scoffed Cathy. But she did dream of John Crowley that night, his fingers tracing the outline of her lips before he kissed her.

Chapter Ten

Cathy filled her weekend with as much fun as she could, and even went rafting Saturday, but spent Sunday as her father had requested, studying. Attacking her algebra homework, she realized how far behind she'd fallen.

At noon, out of desperation, she phoned John. Wouldn't he be pleased she was asking for help?

Nobody was home at his house. Cathy toyed with the notion of phoning Tim, who would come charging over in a flash, but she thought better of it. There was no reason to encourage him when she didn't want him encouraged.

Alone, she sweated out one page of homework, while Monday morning grew menacingly closer with each passing minute.

On Monday Mr. Marcus handed back the test papers. He called out each student's name, and each had to walk up to the front of the class to receive his or her paper. Cathy squirmed in her seat, legs and fingers crossed, waiting. Why she crossed legs and fingers she didn't know—perhaps in the hope that by some miracle there was an A on her paper. The expressions worn by students returning to their seats were evidence of what kinds of grades they had received, and Cathy hoped her face wouldn't betray her in the same way.

"Cathy Meyers."

The clipped, curt way Mr. Marcus read out her name chilled her to the bone. Under the mossy cliff of his eyebrows, his blue eyes pierced her own.

"I expected better from you, Cathy," he remarked in a low voice, so that the knowledge did not have to be shared with the rest of the class.

"I'm sorry," she whispered, dropping her eyes to her paper. Her stomach twisted at the sight of the many check marks, vicious red slashes across the mimeographed sheet, and the fiercely bright D at the top of the paper.

A D minus! Just this side of an F, which, with a little less effort, it could have been.

Cathy felt sick. Angrily she shoved the test

paper into her binder, wishing she could simply crumple it into a tight ball and throw it in the trash. But, of course, she couldn't do that. The algebra test was the first thing her parents would ask about when she arrived home. There was absolutely no way out.

Quick, bitter strides ate up the distance between class and her locker. To Cathy's surprise John was standing in front of her locker. She forgot to wonder how he knew where her locker was.

"What are you doing here?" she demanded.

His brown eyes flicked over her quickly. "I just wondered how you did on your test."

"John, I'm trying to forget what I got on my test, if you don't mind."

He shifted his gaze to his wrist, but seeing he'd forgotten to wear his watch, he looked away. "I was just worried," he explained. "That bad, huh?"

Cathy jerked her head up to face him. Tears ached at the back of her throat. "Yeah. A D minus is pretty bad, isn't it?"

"Cathy," he said with alarm.

"You didn't have to ask, John," she returned coldly, whirling around to face her locker so that he didn't see the one slow tear sliding down her cheek.

John sighed. "I'm sorry, but I was afraid this would happen."

"Cathy, how could you?" was Sybil Meyers' exasperated response as she smoothed the test paper in front of her on the coffee table in the den.

"John worked so hard with you. I'm just terribly disappointed with this grade." Stephen Meyers wore his disappointment in the forward slump of his broad shoulders. He gave a tired sigh. "This is just inexcusable. What are we going to do with you?"

"I don't know. Send me to reform school?" Cathy retorted smartly, dropping into a chair, draping her long legs over one arm.

"Don't be flip, young lady. Your last grade was so promising, and now this. You realize you'll have to work doubly hard to bring your grade average up by the end of the term. This is your last chance."

She knew everything he was saying was correct, but the knowledge only seemed to fuel her contrariness.

"Who cares whether I learn algebra or not? Is it going to scar me for life?" Cathy challenged, out of the corner of her eye catching her mother's flinch. Instantly she knew she'd gone too far, but it was too late, so she bumbled on stupidly. "I'll probably be a dancer or something," she decided in a split second.

"That would be very nice," her dad told her coolly. "But you'll need some sort of education in order to get yourself a job while you're learning dance." He cleared his throat and, with his forefinger, traced the carving on a wooden pencil pot. "If you don't raise this grade by the end of this school year, you'll have to repeat the class in your senior year, which I don't believe you want to do, do you, Cathy?"

She shrugged.

"Mr. Marcus informs me that you have one more important test this semester, and if you do well on it, you'll pass with a C. As I've told you, your high school grades really do matter when you enter college. They are sent to every college you apply to, and who's going to accept you with D's and F's?"

"Lots of people don't go to college," Cathy argued back. "Thomas Edison, William Saroyan, Shakespeare—lots of people."

"That's very true," her father agreed in his calm, classroom voice. "But those people lived in different times. I don't think they had the social life you do. And I don't believe they had the same attitude you have, either."

It was just as well the doorbell interrupted them at that moment because Cathy did not want to be lectured to anymore.

Sybil rose. "That must be John. I'll answer it."

"Saved by the bell," breathed Cathy.

"You might as well just sit here and wait for him, Cathy. He's almost as concerned about your work as we are." Stephen Meyers turned on his heel and marched out, leaving Cathy sitting in the chair, seething.

John entered, carrying his usual burden of books, but this time he dropped a paperback into her lap. "This one's for you," he said. "I thought it might help you." He sat down in another chair.

She read the title: *Overcoming Math Anxiety* by Sheila Tobias. Leave it to John to think that people can solve their problems by reading a book, she thought. "Thanks," she said. "I'll look at it later." Cathy pushed the book aside and smiled up at John. "Besides, I've decided to study dance instead of math. What do you think?"

"Cathy, you're incredible! You've just blown the most important test of the semester, and you're acting like you don't even care!"

"What do you want me to do, cry on your shoulder? Come on. Let's dance. You can't say you don't like it until you try." Cathy stood up and grabbed both his hands and tried to urge him out of his chair, but he refused to budge. He shrank from her, but Cathy wouldn't let go, and to the surprise of both of them, she dropped into his lap.

"Stop it, Cathy," John said roughly, but Cathy paid no attention.

"Your hair is in your eyes," she purred, stroking stray wisps back and hooking her arms around his neck.

Abruptly he shoved her away, got up, and retucked his shirt. "When are you ever going to grow up?" he shouted. "For some stupid reason I keep expecting you to change, but you won't even try. So why do I keep on trying to help you?"

"I don't know. Why do you? It sure was easier getting D's in algebra before you came along. Now I have to work so hard for them—and put up with so much abuse."

"You know what, Cathy? You're absolutely right. I can't help you. When I take a job, I take it seriously, and I'm just not making any progress with you. It's a waste of my time and your parents' money. Don't you agree?" There was a hard edge to his voice that Cathy had never heard before. "I've had it, Cathy. I'm telling your parents I quit."

Cathy swallowed hard. John looked frightningly fierce as he gathered up his things. "I need you, John, don't you see? Please don't quit."

"No. I've made up my mind. You'll manage, one way or another. Goodbye, Cathy."

Helplessly, Cathy watched him leave. Then the realization hit her, spreading like a huge, regretful ache inside her. This time he would never come back. She had really blown it. Suddenly she wished she could call back the words she had said, she wished she had been different with John. There was something about her he couldn't stand, and maybe, maybe she couldn't blame him. Or maybe, as she had suspected all along, he just wasn't her type.

Chapter Eleven

"Okay, Cathy. Tell me what happened?" Sybil Meyers' hands twisted in her apron.

Cathy blew her bangs out of her eyes and sighed innocently. "I don't know, Mom. John just got mad at me for no reason."

Her mother studied her with disbelief. "I don't think that's the whole story. John's put up with a lot from you, young lady. And what gets to me is that you've got everything to lose if you don't buckle down and study."

"Oh, Mom!" Cathy threw up her hands in exasperation. "There are other tutors around, you know. John's not the only one. He and I have a personality clash, that's all. We haven't gotten along since the day we met. I mean, he doesn't have a humorous bone in his body. He's just too serious. All he talks about is math."

"We paid him to talk to you about math, remember? We didn't hire you an entertainer." Her mother pinned her down with a piercing stare.

"Tim Bryant will tutor me. He's already offered."

"I'll bet he has." Sybil frowned, obviously keeping some thoughts to herself. "One thing your father and I decided when we hired a tutor for you was that it was foolish to choose someone you knew socially, because you'd never get any work done.

"But we were wrong about that, too. Obviously it doesn't matter *who* we choose, you will look at him or her as some kind of social conquest." She sighed heavily, wiping a strand of auburn hair from her eyes. "I don't understand you, Cathy. When I was your age, I was never so wrapped up in friends or boyfriends that I neglected my schoolwork. My brothers and I were always taught to see the importance of work before play. I suppose your father and I have been too easy on you."

"Too easy? You're always breathing down my neck. What'll you do with me next? Put me in a straitjacket?"

"Stop it, Cathy." For fear of exchanging further angry words, her mother whirled around and left her.

Cathy was shaken by the whole afternoon. It wasn't her family's way to argue; problems always were solved through sensible conversation. Well, sometimes, like now, she didn't feel sensible; she felt about as unsensible as an eight-year-old—or at least, that's the way everyone was making her feel. Being the only one in a family who voiced opinions loudly, the only one who even *shouted*, was really tough.

"So he quit, huh?" Jan shook her head in amazement at the news. "That's a first for you, Cathy."

"Sounds like things have been popping between you two," commented Tracy wryly.

"I told you we didn't hit it off. He's just way too serious, really drab." Cathy remembered how John's eyes had glittered, sparks flying, as he looked at her. No amount of crooning could cool that fire, she thought now, smiling casually for the benefit of her friends.

But Cathy didn't feel any better for downgrading John. Her unkind remarks didn't diminish John in any way, they only flung her anger out in wider circles. Naturally, her friends were eager to hear what she had to say, and being friends, they took her side. After all, wasn't that what friends were for?

Yet deep down, she felt slimy for talking about him this way, because none of it was really the truth. Sure, he was serious, but that didn't make him ugly. The fact that he didn't succumb to her charms made him all the more attractive. And, he wasn't the least bit drab—in fact, his leanly carved features had become more striking to her the more she saw of them.

"Just a passing interest" was how Cathy described John to Tracy and Jan, and since passing interests were in character for her, they didn't question it, although she did detect a twinkle of doubt in Tracy's eye. Jan simply insisted that Cathy was too pretty and popular to mess around with a boy like John, so it was just as well. There were plenty of boys who were just as smart, but not as single-minded as he, who just loved Cathy.

But in spite of everything and everybody, Cathy secretly looked for John every day at school.

Chapter Twelve

The public library was an ivy-cov-ered stone building that had been standing since before the turn of the century. Because of the rot caused by the ivy, the town council had threatened to tear it down, but no move had been made in that direction because so far, the protests of the Historical Society were continuous, loud, and fierce.

Cathy loved the library, just as it was. There was a pungent, earthy scent pervading the structure, which her dear brother Matt insisted was the smell of the rot. She didn't believe him, though.

But rot or no rot, it was the kind of place Cathy didn't realize she missed until she returned there. She loved the heavy, reverent silence which was broken only by the whisper of turning pages or the operation of the Xerox machine.

Tim reached for Cathy's hand as they climbed the steps to the heavy wooden doors, which he held open for her. She ducked under his arm before the door shut behind them.

"I want to look up something in the *National Geographic*," Cathy said, pointing in the direction of the magazine racks.

"I'm gonna look for some books on Egypt," Tim said.

Cathy looked through several magazines. She enjoyed browsing through publications that she didn't see in the grocery store, like the ones on antiques and *Arizona Highways*, which had beautiful photographs.

She saw Tim between aisles, hunched over an Egypt book, no doubt. Her parents had allowed her to go to the library with him, only on the condition that she study here. Tim quickly assured them that that was all he had in mind. Then Cathy took the opportunity to let him know she was in real need of help on her algebra homework (not mentioning what had happened with John), and Tim was more than happy to oblige her.

"Tim, I hate to bother you, but can you help me find the current issue of the *Geographic?*" she implored.

Tim gazed at her, soft-eyed, nearly dropping the thick picture book he was holding. "Sure," he said. "Be right there." Clumsily, he shoved the book back in the case and followed her over to the magazines.

"Here it is, Cathy, right on the rack."

At that moment Cathy spotted John sitting nearby, leaning over to pick up a fallen book from the carpet. As he straightened, their eyes met and locked. Cathy's breath lodged somewhere between her diaphragm and her throat.

"Oh, hi, John. What a surprise," she whispered.

He smiled uncertainly, and Cathy suddenly remembered Tim at her side.

"Studying?" John asked, cocking his head to one side.

"Uh, yes." Cathy tugged nervously at her hair.

"Hi, John. How're ya doin'?" Tim said.

"Great. How's basketball?"

Cathy was vaguely aware of Tim's response as she watched John watching her. Suddenly she heard Tim saying, "Hope you don't mind if I give your prize pupil a few math lessons myself this afternoon."

"Not at all," John said, looking straight at Cathy. "Didn't she tell you I wasn't tutoring her anymore?"

"Well, no, she didn't." Tim looked flustered and confused, as if he could suddenly feel the electricity between Cathy and John but couldn't quite believe it.

"Let's go, Tim," Cathy said. "We've got lots of work to do, and I'm absolutely *sure* John does too. Right, John?"

"That's right," John said, still staring at Cathy.

"See you later," Cathy said, trying to sound cheerful.

John's big brown eyes looked sad as he watched them walk away. "Goodbye, Cathy," he whispered.

"See ya in trig, John. Take it easy," Tim said, handing Cathy the magazine she had been looking for. He led her to a big round table where he deposited his stack of books. "What's going on between you and John?" he asked Cathy.

"Obviously nothing. He's not even my tutor anymore."

"What happened?"

"We just didn't get along. He's just not my type, you know?"

"What do you mean, not your type? He was only supposed to be helping you with your algebra, right?"

"Right. That was all he was supposed to do," Cathy said, a faraway look in her eyes. "Look, I told you we just didn't get along. I wasn't learning anything. Now, are you going to help me or not?"

"Sure, sure. Take it easy. Where's your homework?"

She pulled out her homework paper. "It's really nice of you to help me with this, Tim. You don't know how much I appreciate it," she said. But her voice did not have the usual effect on him. He did not seem as pleased to be with her as he had a few minutes before.

Cathy felt miserable. She realized she had been mistreating Tim as badly as John. She'd lost the boy she really wanted and was still encouraging someone she didn't really care about. What was wrong with her? That day, her ability to concentrate on algebra was the worst it had ever been.

Chapter Thirteen

"You ought to phone John, Cathy, and tell him that you apologize," her father suggested. "I can see you still need his help."

"Are you kidding? After the way he walked out when I really needed him? I'll never ask John Crowley for help again. I guess I'll just have to pass algebra on my own. But I still don't understand why one of you can't help me. What good is it having teachers for parents if they can't even help you with your homework?"

"My algebra is pretty rusty," admitted Stephen Meyers. "Your mother's better at it than I am."

His wife shot him a questioning look. "Oh?" she remarked, and then: "Well, I suppose we could try." She turned to Cathy. "But I don't think you should give up on John. He's a nice boy, and he needs the money. . . ."

Cathy remembered John saying he needed

money that day they had had the fight in the ice cream parlor, but she couldn't imagine why he needed it. It certainly wasn't for soccer cleats or anything like most of the boys she knew would use it for. He didn't play sports. He had no fancy car or clothes to maintain—was relatively conservative in dress and rode that old bike everywhere; he probably even fixed it himself.

Just another one of her mother's excuses to get her sympathy, she decided. "If he needs the money, then why did he quit?" Cathy asked. "It wasn't my idea."

Her mother's appeal on John's behalf rose and fell, a backdrop for Cathy's thoughts. What was it her mom had said was wrong with John's father? He'd had some kind of surgery and was recuperating, which meant virtually nothing to Cathy. Nobody in her family had ever undergone any serious surgery. One summer Matt had had his tonsils out and was allowed to eat a disgusting amount of ice cream, but other than that, everyone had al-ways been in perfect health.

As she bent over her algebra book, Cathy's mind meandered back to John, the sun picking up deep reddish highlights in his dark hair, and the rough but silky way his skin felt against hers. She imagined that if he ever put his arms around her, his embrace would be gentle, considerate.

Just why did he fascinate her so? Was it because *he* played hard to get (she thought she'd cornered the market with that game), or because his wasn't a game at all, but just plain serious business? He had no time for her games—or for her. Every other boy she'd ever met had all the time in the world for her. They fell over their feet for the opportunity to sit next to her. She knew just what to say and do to attract them.

For a few days, Tim Bryant had phoned her to see how she was doing and to see if she needed any help with her algebra. But she had gently discouraged him, and he seemed to have taken the hint. She was relieved now that it was all over.

During the next week, Cathy came straight home from school each day to work with her mother for an hour on algebra. Sybil Meyers kicked off her clogs and touched the textbook as if it were a Ouija board that could magically give her the answers.

"It's been so long since I've done this," she mused. "I'm so accustomed to second grade math."

"That's about where I am, too, Mom." Cathy

proceeded to explain what she barely understood herself. "See? Even you have to admit you're not using it in your life. How many times do you run across an algebra problem?"

"Not too often. But having this knowledge does offer you more career choices in life. It's required, and it's supposed to make you into a more well-rounded individual."

"Well rounded—ha! And we're all trying to go on diets."

Her mother laughed. Cathy had always thought of her mother as a happy person. She never complained about anything. But she also kept to herself a lot, so it was sometimes hard to tell what she was thinking and feeling. But in those hours they spent together muddling out the algebra, Cathy learned a few things about her mother.

Her mother approached math the way she approached other challenges in her life. She had a real curiosity about it and seemed to want to reach out and take hold of it, turn it around, and see why it worked as it did. The results didn't quite match John's, but Cathy had to admit that her mother's spirit and determination put her own efforts to shame.

Sybil Meyers also had endless patience, but even patience couldn't solve some of Cathy's algebra problems. Finally, completely stumped, Sybil quietly laid down her pencil. "I'm sorry, Cathy. I don't know where to begin with these problems. We've got to call John to help you."

"Never! I don't want you to call him. If you can't help me, I'll just have to do it myself."

"Cathy, what happened between you and John? He's such a nice boy. Why did you have to give him such a hard time?"

"I just tried to help him loosen up a little. He could be a really popular guy if he weren't so serious all the time. But whenever I tried to talk to him, we ended up in an argument. It was weird."

Her mother smiled. "Your father and I used to have arguments like that sometimes. But *I* was the serious one. I really hated it when he tried to make me lighten up."

"You and Dad used to have arguments? I can't believe it."

"Oh, we still do sometimes, but I guess we're so used to each other's ways—and we've learned to compromise. If you care about someone, you make an effort to understand and bend a little bit. You'll find that out some day."

Cathy was amazed to hear her mother telling her so much about herself. "Thanks, Mom," she said and meant it.

"Sorry I couldn't be more help with algebra," her mother said, smiling as she walked away. "Think again about calling John, okay?"

"Okay. I'll think about it." Alone again in her room, Cathy took a fresh sheet of paper out of her desk drawer, determined to figure out the rest of the problems. When she shut the drawer, a pile of books and binders toppled off the desk top onto the floor.

She leaned down to scoop them up and discovered *Overcoming Math Anxiety*—the book John had given her the night he had quit. She'd never even opened it. It had been lying under a mound of papers on her desk. But now she was curious. Maybe some of her attitudes *were* holding her back and messing up her life. Maybe there were some changes she could make if she wanted to.

She sat down and read a chapter, then two. There was a direct link between mathematics and vocational opportunities, Cathy found out. Even high school math programs had a great influence on future careers. Traditionally, math had been considered a male subject, according to the author, and women were generally encouraged into nonmath subjects such as humanities, teaching, nursing, and social work.

Cathy thought of her parents, who had always encouraged her to tackle anything she might find interesting. She could now see that she was cutting off her own choices if she didn't at least give math a chance. Maybe there was something to this "math anxiety" stuff, but the important thing tonight was just to get her homework done.

As she was closing the paperback, something caught her eye. On the second page was an inscription: *For Cathy, the girl who has everything, plus a lot of potential to be anything she really wants to be. Love, John Crowley.*

Gasping, Cathy read it over and over again. John had written this for *her!* He had cared enough to write this, and she had never even opened the book before today!

She set the paperback aside and tried to finish her homework. But John's face blanked out the equations; his brown eyes locked with her own. Tomorrow, she would start working on her math anxiety. Tonight, she day-dreamed she was in John Crowley's arms, and he was telling her things he'd always wanted to tell her. . . .

The next day she looked for John at school but he wasn't there. She was very quiet all day, and Jan and Tracy couldn't figure out what was going on.

"Looks like algebra has finally done her in," Jan said.

"Either algebra or John Crowley," Tracy said, smiling.

John must be sick, Cathy thought. I'll find out where he lives and stop by his house after school. If I call him, he'll just say he doesn't want to see me.

When she got home, she looked up John's number in her mother's directory. The address, 41 Pine Street, stared up at her. Should she, or shouldn't she visit him? Maybe she could ask him out for a Coke. That way, he would have to hear her out, wouldn't he?

There was so much she wanted to get straight with him, even if he wasn't interested in tutoring her.

Quickly she dressed in a pair of nice jeans and a cream-colored blouse. She pulled her bike out from behind the garbage cans and headed for his house.

When she got to John's, his black bike was nowhere in sight. Perhaps he parked it in the back yard. But if he isn't there, she wondered, should I wait?

Simple decisions like this had never been a

problem to Cathy before. She had always played everything by ear, and one way or another, everything always had worked out. But with John, her methods hadn't worked that well. Everything seemed so crucial now. He might not like her being here. He might be turned off—he might reject her. Cathy had never had to deal with that, and she didn't know if she could now.

Mentally reviewing what she might say, Cathy took a deep breath and knocked at the front door.

The house was in an older section of town, where many homes were being renovated, and it was set apart from its neighbors by the pleasing contrast of its white and brick-red paint job. A low brick wall planter housed a profusion of flowers, and a huge maple tree dominated one side of the front lawn. A boy of about Matt's age vaulted onto a bike and hurtled out of the driveway, a newspaper sack slung across one shoulder.

"Oh, hi. Who are you?" From the open doorway a pigtailed girl Cathy guessed to be around ten blinked at her questioningly.

"I'm Cathy Meyers," she answered, smiling. "I'm a friend of John's. Is he home?"

"John?" The girl sounded surprised, and

haltingly added, "He's not here right now. Why don't you come in and wait?"

Cathy hesitated. What would John think of her waiting for him? It wasn't really her style to wait for boys—they usually had to wait for her.

The little girl watched her expectantly for an answer, so she finally agreed to come inside.

"I'm Lucy," the girl introduced herself, guiding Cathy through cool, dark hallways. Judging by the maze of hallways, several rooms had been added onto the original structure over the years. Cathy could tell by her brief introduction that the home was quite comfortable, sort of like her own.

"Do you and John go to the same school?" asked Lucy, surveying Cathy through a pair of brown eyes nearly identical to John's.

"Yes. He used to tutor me," Cathy ventured, not knowing what John had told his family about her. "He wasn't in school today, so I came by to see if he's all right."

"Oh, so you're the one." Lucy seemed to study her with new interest. "I always wondered what you looked like. You're so pretty. Don't worry about John. He's not sick. But he has been getting pretty tired lately, so my father let him sleep late today. He's picking up my mother from work right now."

"We have a visitor, Lucy?" A deep, male voice preceded its owner into the room. A man in a wheelchair rolled into the room. His eyes lit up when he caught sight of Cathy. "Well, well. Hello," he greeted her, extending a large, workworn hand. His handshake was firm. "I'm J.D. Crowley. And who might you be?" J.D. winked at her.

She introduced herself quite formally, telling him that she went to John's school. "I heard you had surgery recently," she continued. "I'm sorry." She didn't know whether or not sorry was the right thing to say.

"Yes, I am too, but it beats the pain of broken parts. Surgery's amazing nowadays. They can fuse your bones together. Did you know that?" He quickly shrugged it off before Cathy could respond. "Of course, you wouldn't be interested in that. An old man's grumblings about his operation."

"Oh, no," she protested, for she didn't think of him as old. She guessed he was about her father's age. "It sounds really interesting. I didn't know that they could do that."

"Would you like something to drink?" he asked. Cathy nodded, and Lucy went off to the kitchen. "Lucy and I are the only ones here right now. Lucy's my nurse, you see." He winked again. "My wife Mary works at the hospital, my daughter Jennifer has a job in a boutique, and Chad has a paper route. John had a tutoring job and will be getting another soon. So you know John?"

"Yes," Cathy said. "I wanted to talk to him about something."

A sudden wince of pain flitted almost imperceptibly across Mr. Crowley's face, but it didn't interfere with his interest in Cathy. "Oh?"

Not wanting to tell John's father that she was the person John had been tutoring, Cathy was relieved that Lucy reentered the room at that moment and said, "Here's some lemonade." She gave tall glasses of pink lemonade to her father and to Cathy. Cathy thought she seemed awfully adult for her young years.

"Thanks, Lucy."

They sat in the dining room, where several woodworking projects were in various stages of completion. There was a round table top with four curvy legs lying next to it. Mr. Crowley noticed Cathy looking at them.

"John found those legs at the flea market,"

he explained. "I'm making a table top for 'em, and Mary will stain it, and it'll be one expensive-looking piece of furniture."

"Take a look at this." He wheeled his chair over to a rocker that was minus its rockers. "We had to carve new rockers for this baby. We'll put some oak stain on her, and she'll look as good as new."

Cathy was accustomed to flea markets and garage sales, since her mother's idea of fun was picking over somebody else's musty cast-offs. But she had never seen secondhand furniture refinished as beautifully as Mr. Crowley's, and she told him so.

"My mom collects a few old things, but she doesn't know how to repair and redo them like you do," she said. As she took a better look around, she saw that there were many more lovely things. "Did you do all these pieces?"

"Most of them," J.D. answered proudly. "That clawfooted table, for instance. Had to scrape about five layers of paint off it before we found the wood. But look how pretty it came up."

"And that cabinet is my pride and joy," he went on, picking out other objects in the room, relating their history. Cathy lost track of time, as though she were being given a museum tour. Old hurricane lamps, a gossip bench, tea cart, rockers, and an heirloom hope chest she just knew her mother would love.

"And look at this." Lucy emerged from the hall toting a doll bed of very old wicker, painted white. Hidden beneath folds of frothy, yellowed lace was a china doll with a mended face.

"How pretty," exclaimed Cathy, and she was genuinely surprised at herself for thinking so. Her mother had brought home a doll much like this one when she had been very little. An old doll with a cracked face and torn, dirty clothes. Cathy had hated it and thought it was horribly ugly. Her mother had wanted to fix it up, but Cathy didn't want it, so it was given to an aunt in Oregon.

It could've been a beautiful doll, Cathy thought now, if only I'd given it a chance. Why don't I ever give things a chance?

The late afternoon sun slanted into the living room, right across Mr. Crowley's face. Lucy had gone to her room, so Cathy jumped up to adjust the shades. "Relax, young lady, I won't melt, you know."

"Please let me make myself useful while I'm here, Mr. Crowley. Can I get anything for you while I'm up?"

"Well, you might grab the bottle of pills in the cabinet above the sink and bring a glass of water with them, if you don't mind."

"Of course I don't mind."

When she returned, Mr. Crowley thanked her and said, "I suppose John's caught in traffic, Cathy. I thought he'd be home by now. You know, my family has really been pitching in since my accident. I'm pretty useless to them right now."

"Useless? How can you say that after showing me all the beautiful things you've restored? What kind of work did you do for a living?" Cathy asked.

"I was a welder," he said, and seeing her confused look, he explained, "A guy who sews metal together."

"Oh." She flushed at her ignorance. "How did you hurt your back?"

"Metal pipe fell on my spine," he said matter-of-factly.

"Oh." That was all Cathy could say. She just couldn't imagine anything so horrible happening to someone she knew.

"It's not a nice thing to remember. But I'm a very lucky man. I know that."

"You're a very *special* man, Mr. Crowley. I can see now where John gets his determination."

"You sound like you know John pretty well. But he doesn't talk about girls much at home . . . and they certainly don't come to visit him very often," he said, chuckling. "He'll be jealous of his old dad for keeping you to myself."

Cathy blushed. "I'm not so sure of that." She changed the subject abruptly. "You know, I think it's really great the way you can fix things up. I keep thinking of that china doll. I never would have suspected how beautiful it could be. And it's all because of your patience and your skill—and your love for things, isn't it? Do you think—do you think maybe I could come by sometime and watch you when you're restoring something? I'd really like to learn how to do it."

"Come by any time you like," Mr. Crowley said, smiling. "I'm sure John will second the invitation."

"Thank you, Mr. Crowley. Now I'm afraid I'll have to be going. My mother will have a fit if I'm late for dinner. Please tell John I'm very sorry I missed him."

"John will be sorry he missed you, I'm sure."

"Goodbye, Mr. Crowley. Goodbye, Lucy," she called. "See you soon." Cathy hopped onto her bike, with a new and valuable knowledge of John Crowley in her heart.

Chapter Fourteen

She had been wrong about John all along, thinking he was boring and too seri-ous. Life *was* serious to him. It wasn't one great long party as it was for her.

Since his father's injury, Cathy guessed that nothing had come too easily to the Crowleys. The entire family, including little Lucy, was pitching in to make everything run just as smoothly as ever. Their quiet humor and sense of togetherness surprised and warmed Cathy.

Suddenly, she felt ashamed of herself for the way she'd acted—toward John and to-ward her parents. She had placed too much emphasis on being popular and having fun. Of course, John had tried to tell her that in his own way, but she hadn't been willing to listen.

She had breezed through life with such ease! The road she had traveled had been completely smooth, but it couldn't be that way for everyone, and it might not continue to be that easy for her, either, she realized. Now that she had met John and his father, she knew that life would never seem quite so simple to her again.

How silly and frivolous I've been! she thought, pedaling vigorously down the hill to her house. Of course, I still think John has something to learn about having fun, and maybe I could teach him if he'd let me. But I certainly haven't gone about it very wisely so far.

How could she change? Cathy had been Cathy for as long as she could remember. There were not too many other personalities she could readily adopt. Maybe she would just have to settle for shaving off the rough edges of her character for now.

Smiling to herself, she coasted into the garage, nearly hitting Matt as he stepped out the kitchen door.

"Where've you been?" he demanded. The frayed T-shirt he wore was smeared with jelly and grease.

Cathy whirled him around, and he fought to extricate himself from her grasp. "I just went over to a friend's."

"Mom's looking for you, you goon," Matt grumbled, climbing onto his decal-plastered go-cart.

"Cathy, where have you been?" Sybil looked up from the pile of workbooks she was correcting.

"I just went over to John's," she blurted out.

Sybil Meyers tried hard to conceal a smile. "Oh? Do you think you might like to make some tea and tell me about it?" She laid down her pen and tucked a wisp of auburn hair back into its bun.

"Yeah, okay, Mom." While she made tea, Cathy told her mother all about John's father, the expertly refinished collectibles that her mother would absolutely love, and Lucy.

"I told you John's family was having a hard time." Her mother sighed. "Your grandfather had back trouble, you know. But I guess you just have to see things for yourself. No one can tell you anything."

Cathy set out cream, sugar, and the teapot. "Do you think he might reconsider tutoring, Mom?" she asked, pouring an amber stream into her mother's cup.

Her mother studied her closely. "It depends on why you want him to reconsider. John's not about to waste his time—but you can try, Cathy," she said encouragingly. "You've just got to show him that you mean it about working."

Just then, the doorbell rang. It was a crazy chime that Sybil had picked up at a flea market and Stephen had repaired.

With a swish of her ruffled skirt, Sybil Meyers answered the door.

"Oh, John, come on in. I have your check."

Cathy's heart leaped into her throat. She hurried into the front hall, putting on her best smile. "Hi, John," she said shyly.

John shoved his fingers in his front pockets. "Hi, Cathy. How are you?"

"Oh, fine." Cathy leaned against the doorjamb, at a loss for words for the first time in her life. Her mother rustled off to get John's check, her voice trailing behind her.

"Won't you sit down with us and have some tea, John? Cathy just made some."

"Oh—uh—no, thank you. I'd better be getting back." He glanced sheepishly at Cathy.

Impulsively she reached out and touched his arm. "John, wait," she whispered. He flinched. "I wanted to tell you I'm sorry for causing you trouble. I didn't realize, I mean—just accept my apology, will you?"

He nodded, his smile tentative. "Okay."

"And, John, I wanted to tell you I finally read that book you brought me. And I've learned a few things since I saw you last—about algebra and about John Crowley."

He blushed deeply and said nothing. But the stiffness seemed to have left his posture, so she felt it safe to continue. "What I really want to ask you is, would you consider tutoring me again?" Cathy watched his face shift as he thought about the question. *Say yes,* she wished, hoping her brain waves would reach out and influence him.

John bit his lower lip, obviously thinking it over very carefully. That was John—careful, cautious. Cathy bet he never jumped into anything.

Do you know what, John? You look just like that Rodin statue of The Thinker. You really do. All serious and thoughtful. She held back her own feelings, waiting for his answer.

"Let me think it over, okay, Cathy?"

Expectation slid from her face, tinkling down somewhere inside her like shattered glass. Think it over! What was there to think over? Her pride rose up in mute surprise. Numbly, she muttered, "Oh, sure. Uh, think it over."

Her mother returned with John's check.

"I'm sorry I can't stay," John addressed her. "I'd better get going."

Sybil's smile was expansive. "Thanks so much, John. And don't make a stranger of yourself."

"I won't. And thank you." He indicated the check, then turned to Cathy, who was pretending to be engrossed in a painting on the wall that she'd only stared at thousands of times before. She was thinking: maybe now he'll change his mind and say yes.

"I'll think about it, Cathy, and let you know," was what he said.

She turned and nodded, speechless, angry at herself for bothering to ask him at all.

That night at dinner, Cathy was as quiet as her family had ever seen her. Fortunately, even Matt seemed to respect her feelings for once, and nobody pressed her to take part in the conversation. As they were finishing dessert, the phone rang, and Matt ran to answer it.

"Oh, yeah, she's here. Hi, John. How're ya doing?" Matt made a face at his sister as he handed her the phone.

Cathy felt a knot in her stomach. She hoped her voice wasn't shaking as she said, "Hi, John. How are you?"

"I'm fine. How about you?"

"Fine."

"My dad told me you stopped by."

"Yeah. I liked your family."

"That was nice of you—to come by, that is."

Now that all the amenities had been spoken, what else did they talk about? Cathy felt sudden panic. Here it is, proof absolute that we are too different—John and I have nothing in common except a discussion of the weather and our health.

After a lengthy, awkward silence, John cleared his throat and said, "Listen, Cathy, I thought over your offer, and decided that I would come back and tutor you. But"—his voice held a note of reservation—"I can't put up with your kidding around. Otherwise, we're just wasting our time."

Cathy smiled into the receiver. *You've got my undivided attention, John—I can't think of anything else!* "You've got it," she announced brightly. "I told you, I'm sorry for how I behaved." She was going to add, "it was inexcusable," but decided against it. There was such a thing as laying it on too thick, which John would be suspicious of. She must be careful not to drive him away again.

"We'll start, let's see—what time is good for you?"

Anytime—tonight, she nearly blurted out but checked herself. She was supposed to be going skating that night, anyway. But she could cancel that. "Tonight?"

"Tonight I've got a meeting of the chess club. How about tomorrow, after school? Say around four?"

So he was the one who was busy, Cathy thought. Were the tables turning?

"Oh, sure," she replied, glad he couldn't see the stunned expression on her face. "That would be fine."

Cathy hung up and did cartwheels down the hall, her joy bubbling up inside her like an oil gusher.

"Yippee!" she squealed as she whirled past Matt, who frowned at her with disdain.

"What a jerk," he commented. "You're really out of it, Cathy. Shall I call the little men in white coats?"

"Call anyone you want, Matt," she cried gaily, backflipping onto her bed.

Chapter Fifteen

John stretched his arm along the backrest behind Cathy as she worked on her homework. She imagined his arm tightening around her shoulders, his lips against hers, the algebra book sliding off her lap and onto the floor with a muffled thump.

But that didn't happen. She had to concentrate. There wasn't much time left until the end of school and report card time, and she had to use what was left to the fullest—no fooling around.

It was funny how, since John had begun tutoring her again, her brain had opened up and she really felt like she was learning something. Maybe it was the book he'd given her that was helping, too, showing her the importance of what she was studying.

"You've been working so hard, Cathy," John said, checking her answers. "I'm really impressed. It shows."

"Really? That book you gave me really helped. I decided I didn't want to be among the majority of girls who have a math avoidance problem," she told him knowledgeably.

John looked amused. "I don't blame you. Why let the boys enjoy all the math subjects?" He glanced back at her paper. "You got all of these right."

"You're not seeing a mirage, are you?" she inquired sweetly. She had been ever so careful not to tease him, biting her lip when the wild comments threatened to burst forth. After all, he was probably pretty wary of her by now.

"No. It's perfect. Congratulations."

John's elbows were propped on the arms of the chair, and he looked relaxed. Cathy wanted to hug him, but instead, she said, "Thank you. But I couldn't have done it without you, John. You know that."

He threw back his head and let out an unrestrained laugh that surprised Cathy.

"What's wrong? What did I say?" she prodded. "I mean, it's nice to see you laugh once in awhile, but not at me!"

"You're so funny, you know that?" He laughed again. "You only needed someone to show you that you could do it. You've been acting like I was going to bite you for a week now, and I can't understand it. When have I ever been a threat to you, Cathy?"

She felt herself blush. "Now you're embarrassing me, John," she replied. "I've only been concentrating on my algebra."

"You haven't been flirting with me or trying any of your usual tricks." John shook his head, pushing up his glasses with one finger. "Gosh, I wonder what happened to the old Cathy. She was a lot of fun."

"What are you getting at?"

"I don't suppose the old Cathy might like to take in a movie tonight, would she? That is, if her parents allow her to go out with her tutor." His ears turned a pale shade of pink. "And we could bring the new Cathy along, too, just to keep the old Cathy under control."

Cathy socked him lightly in the shoulder. "Now you're making fun of me. You make me sound like a split personality. How would you like it if—"

He cut her off. "Come on, it's my turn to make the jokes. Do you want to go to a movie, or not?"

"What do you want to see? A documentary?"

"That doesn't sound bad, but I know something better. Do you like comedies?"

"Of course I do! What do you think I am, anyway? A girl without a sense of humor?" Faintly, she remembered once thinking John had no sense of humor.

"I don't know," he said, his expression deadpan. "You haven't been that much fun lately."

Cathy rose, folded her homework paper, and laid it on the desk. "Well, that's really something, John Crowley, coming from you." She pulled her hair back into a ponytail and wound a rubber band around it.

"Is it a date, or not?"

Cathy noted his confident stance, leaning against her father's desk, and wondered what had happened to him. She shook her head. "What a way to ask for a date, John. You're going to have to learn how to talk to girls. Do you want me to teach you?" she cooed over her shoulder.

"Oh, I don't know about that," John shrugged, on his way out the door. "I think I'm doing okay."

Cathy ran down the hall, yelling after him, "What's that supposed to mean? John? John?"

He didn't answer, leaving her to wonder.

Chapter Sixteen

Two weeks later, on the last day of school, Cathy and John went out again, this time to celebrate: report cards had been given out that day, and Cathy had managed to pass algebra with a B minus. "We did it!" she had ex-claimed when she met John after school. "We really did it!"

That evening they went out to the fanciest restaurant in town and then to a movie. Over dinner, Cathy tried teasing John just a little. "What's happened to you, John? You seem so different lately."

"I guess that's a compliment," he said, a twinkle in his eyes, "since you always hated the way I was before."

"I didn't hate you. I just didn't understand you very well. Actually, I still don't."

"Well, I guess I've learned something from you, Cathy." He looked at her slyly.

She grinned. "Really? You learned something from me? I thought you knew everything."

"Not quite . . . I'm just a beginner when it comes to romance, you know."

Cathy smiled at him, excitement quivering insider her. "Maybe I can still teach you to dance," she suggested. "Do you want to learn?"

He grimaced. "I told you I can't dance. I don't want to make a fool of myself."

"Who's going to let you do that? Are you afraid of making mistakes?" she challenged.

"Well, no—I guess not." He searched for words to explain himself. "I'm just not the dancing type, Cathy. Maybe that part of your life should remain separate from me."

"What for?" demanded Cathy. "What's wrong with a good dance and party once in awhile?"

"I'm not a party person. I like quieter things."

"Ugh. Like chess? Practicing Spanish?" she taunted.

"Cathy," John said gently, "why don't we discuss this later, okay?"

"All right," she agreed sighing.

Later, at the movie, another comedy, Cathy really enjoyed watching John laugh. At certain parts of the movie, tears ran down his face, and she became more entranced in him than in the movie.

At one point, John's arm stole around the back of Cathy's chair, his hand close to her shoulder. Cathy held her breath. Most boys were so anxious to get their arm around you in a dark theater, but not John. His arm lingered on the seat back, and his hand brushed her arm lightly, then moved away.

Cathy was a little disappointed. She wanted him to run his fingers through her hair or squeeze her shoulder. Why was he still holding back?

Rarely did she long for affection or attention. But John's behavior toward her was so puzzling, so different, she couldn't be sure of his true feelings. And, Cathy realized, she was slightly panic-stricken to find that John was the first and only boy she had ever felt vaguely serious about. She had vowed never to feel this way about anyone. She didn't want to fall for John. Why couldn't he simply be like other boys? Why did he have to have so much power over her feelings?

Cathy couldn't bear to have the evening come to an end. It seemed like the most important night of her life, and she wanted it to last a little longer.

"Come on in for a little while," she said. "I think there's some ice cream in the fridge. Let's stuff ourselves."

As they sat on the living room couch, eating their ice cream, John became suddenly shy again. He was startled when Cathy jumped up, put a record on the stereo, and said, "Okay, Crowley, this is it. It's about time I taught you how to dance."

He eyed her warily.

"No, really, I won't do anything. I promise. I just—"She held her slim arms out to him, and he took her hands cautiously, glancing at the pearl ring she wore on her index finger.

"Nice ring," he said, clearing his throat.

Cathy tried to whirl him around, but he stood rooted to the floor. "John, why don't you move? You're like a tree."

"Upright," he stated solemnly.

"Well, okay, but that doesn't help when you're learning to dance. Now come on. I don't know how to lead, I only know how to follow." Her voice dropped to a husky whisper because she didn't want to disturb her parents.

She led John around the floor, chanting, "one-two-three-four, one-two-three-four." John shuffled, stepped on her feet, muttered several apologies, but Cathy persisted, insisting he was doing great.

Cathy thought she felt John's arms tighten against her back (was she imagining it?), and she closed her eyes, allowing the music to move the two of them across the floor, sliding gently in and out of rhythm as John lost his footing, then quickly regained it. She felt his breath against her ear, sending delicious tingles down the back of her neck.

John was holding her close for the first time, and it was just as wonderful as she had dreamed it would be. She knew now she would never grow tired of John Crowley. The boy she had once thought was so boring would never bore her, she realized.

John held her at arm's length and looked at her intently.

"What did you think of me the first time we met?" Cathy asked.

He answered right away. "I thought, 'How in the world am I going to keep my mind on algebra. She's the prettiest girl I've ever met.'"

Cathy giggled and buried her head in the hollow of his shoulder. "Do you know what I thought of you?"

"I can imagine." He winced.

"I thought, 'I'll never be able to loosen this guy up.'"

"I think you mentioned that once." John laughed, drawing her to him. "You sure made it hard for me to keep my mind on the job. And I really did want to help you, you know. You were so darn relentless—and irresistible—you drove me crazy."

"Irresistible? You sure managed to resist me long enough."

"That was for your own good," he teased. "What do you think of me now?"

"I think . . . " Cathy paused, wondering, *can I say what I really feel for him without being hurt?* Then, gazing into his sincere, expectant face, she knew she could trust him. "I think you're the only person, besides my family, that is, that I've ever really cared about."

There, she'd said it—she was trembling.

John stared at her in surprise. "Really? Are you being truthful, Cathy? I mean, you've dated so many popular boys, and I'm just—"

"I'm being truthful, cross my heart." Numbly she traced her finger over her heart. "I've never wanted to like anyone too much."

"And you do now. Is that what I hear you saying?"

She nodded, feeling as if she had just spilled the entire contents of her heart before him, ready to be mopped up any way he pleased.

"Well, I'll admit that I thought caring for you was completely hopeless." John smiled as he held her. "I thought you'd never like me, and I was crazy about you. I've never really looked at girls much before—I mean, I've always been sort of afraid to get involved, myself. Having a girlfriend also seemed so—complicated, especially with the way things are at home for me."

Cathy was about to ask him how he could possibly think she didn't care for him, after all she'd done to get him to notice her, but he was looking directly into her eyes and saying, "I guess we are alike in some ways, Cathy, that we never even suspected."

"You'd never guess that to look at us, John. We're about as mismatched as Mutt and Jeff."

"More like yellow phosphorus and water, actually."

"John! What in the world is *that* supposed to mean?"

"The phosphorus ignites when it hits water," he said, kisses punctuating his words.

"You mean, we're fireworks?"

"Something like that," he murmured, his lips moving over hers so softly and gently that Cathy forgot anything else she might say.

Sweet Dreams®

No.	Code	Title	Author
20323	1	P.S. I LOVE YOU (1)	Barbara Conklin
20325	8	THE POPULARITY PLAN (2)	Rosemary Vernon
20327	4	LAURIE'S SONG (3)	Suzanne Rand
20328	2	PRINCESS AMY (4)	Melinda Pollowitz
20326	6	LITTLE SISTER (5)	Yvonne Greene
20324	X	CALIFORNIA GIRL (6)	Janet Quin-Harkin
20604	4	GREEN EYES (7)	Suzanne Rand
20601	X	THE THOROUGHBRED (8)	Joanna Campbell
20744	X	COVER GIRL (9)	Yvonne Greene
20745	8	LOVE MATCH (10)	Janet Quin-Harkin
20787	3	THE PROBLEM WITH LOVE (11)	Rosemary Vernon
20788	1	NIGHT OF THE PROM (12)	Debra Spector
17779	6	THE SUMMER JENNY FELL IN LOVE (13)	Barbara Conklin
17780	X	DANCE OF LOVE (14)	Jocelyn Saal
17781	8	THINKING OF YOU (15)	Jeanette Nobile
17782	6	HOW DO YOU SAY GOODBYE? (16)	Margaret Burman
17783	4	ASK ANNIE (17)	Suzanne Rand
17784	2	TEN BOY SUMMER (18)	Janet Quin-Harkin
17791	5	LOVE SONG (19)	Anne Park
17792	3	THE POPULARITY SUMMER (20)	Rosemary Vernon
17793	1	ALL'S FAIR IN LOVE (21)	Jeanne Andrews
17794	X	SECRET IDENTITY (22)	Joanna Campbell
17797	4	FALLING IN LOVE AGAIN (23)	Barbara Conklin
17800	8	THE TROUBLE WITH CHARLIE (24)	Joan Lowery Nixon
17795	8	HER SECRET SELF (25)	Rhondi Vilott
17796	6	IT MUST BE MAGIC (26)	Marian Woodruff
17798	2	TOO YOUNG FOR LOVE (27)	Gailanne Maravel
17801	6	TRUSTING HEARTS (28)	Jocelyn Saal
17813	X	NEVER LOVE A COWBOY (29)	Jesse Dukore
17814	8	LITTLE WHITE LIES (30)	Lois I. Fisher
17839	3	TOO CLOSE FOR COMFORT (31)	Debra Spector
17840	7	DAYDREAMER (32)	Janet Quin-Harkin
17841	5	DEAR AMANDA (33)	Rosemary Vernon
17842	3	COUNTRY GIRL (34)	Melinda Pollowitz
17843	1	FORBIDDEN LOVE (35)	Marian Woodruff
17844	X	SUMMER DREAMS (36)	Barbara Conklin
17846	6	PORTRAIT OF LOVE (37)	Jeanette Nobile

17847 4	RUNNING MATES (38)	Jocelyn Saal
17848 2	FIRST LOVE (39)	Debra Spector
17849 0	SECRETS (40)	Anna Aaron
17850 4	THE TRUTH ABOUT ME AND BOBBY V (41)	Janetta Johns
17851 2	THE PERFECT MATCH (42)	Marian Woodruff
17850 2	TENDER LOVING CARE (43)	Anne Park
17853 9	LONG DISTANCE LOVE (44)	Jesse Dukore
17069 4	DREAM PROM (45)	Margaret Burman
17070 8	ON THIN ICE (46)	Jocelyn Saal
17071 6	TE AMO MEANS I LOVE YOU (47)	Deborah Kent
17072 4	DIAL L FOR LOVE (48)	Marian Woodruff
17073 2	TOO MUCH TO LOSE (49)	Suzanne Rand
17074 0	LIGHTS, CAMERA, LOVE (50)	Gailanne Maravel

NON-FICTION TITLES

17859 8	THE SWEET DREAMS BEAUTIFUL HAIR BOOK	Courtney Dewitt
17838 5	THE LOVE BOOK	Deidre Laiken and Alan Schneider
17845 8	THE BODY BOOK	Deidre Laiken and Alan Schneider

If Polly follows her heart, will she lose her best friend* and *her most cherished dream . . .

DANCE OF LOVE

Jocelyn Saal

Ever since third grade, Polly and Jennifer have shared everything from ballet lessons to boy talk. They both dream of becoming famous dancers . . . and falling in love. Then Polly meets Cott Townsend, and her plans get turned upside down. Can Polly win Cott's love, keep Jennifer's friendship and still be true to herself?

Is Fran too smart to fall in love . . .

THINKING OF YOU

Jeanette Nobile

Fran's tired of being called a "brain" . . . and missing all the fun! She wants to be like everyone else for a change – go to parties, have dates, and fall in love.
Can she get Paul to notice her . . . change her image just a little . . . and still be herself?